"I grew up in the Catholic church. On a very basic level, my faith and my love for the teachings of Jesus have always been with me in some form—at times, they've taken the form of a question, and even doubt. But all the same, they're with me. And for many years, I've also been drawn to the idea of a common humanity, common spirituality, the places where different faiths converge. This is an area that has to be approached with great care, charting a just path toward common ground. This is what I value in Tracy Cochran's writings, in *Parabola*, and now in this remarkable book."

—MARTIN SCORSESE, filmmaker

"Through her vivid storytelling and personal sharing, Tracy shares insights from her own journey as an offering for all those on the path to awakening."

—SHARON SALZBERG, author of *Lovingkindness* and *Real Life*

"This is a wonderful, wise, and tender book. Its elegant and gifted storytelling will change you—softening your heart, opening you to the gifts and beauty around you, bringing you into a presence that we so need in this fast-paced world."

—JACK KORNFIELD, author of *A Path with Heart*

"Tracy Cochran offers her readers beautifully written stories filled with delightful anecdotes, poignant insights, and deep wisdom, lovingly encouraging us all in the art of living. She seamlessly weaves contemplations on personal and collective history with reflections on magic and spirituality, allowing her prose to highlight the ultimate beauty and mystery of life. Tracy is a trustworthy guide, leading us through the wondrous mix of the mundane and the mystical at the heart of what it means to be human."

—SEBENE SELA

"Patient teacher and listener. Common soldier. Sharp and wry observer. Practical guide. Fellow seeker. Teller of tales. Keeper of knowledge. Diviner of the good. Pursuer and explorer of mysteries. Doctor of the spirit. The author of these pages, as you will see, is all of these things at once. Alongside the books I turn to for illumination, I can now add Tracy Cochran's *Presence*."

—KENT JONES, filmmaker and writer

"Mindfulness is to be attentive, aware of not just the body, emotions, and thoughts, but the vast interconnected world that surrounds us. Telling stories of her own life journey, writer and meditation teacher Tracy Cochran awakens us to life's moment-by-moment wonder and the teachings that come from what is both ordinary and extraordinary. She guides us to being fully present in our experience, reconnecting us to the deeper roots that can sustain us in our broken world. *Presence* takes us on a journey through darkness and light to an openness to life in the here and now. An invaluable reminder of our original self."

—LLEWELLYN VAUGHAN-LEE, Sufi teacher and
author of *Spiritual Ecology*

"This is a compelling and transformative collection of life stories. The title—*Presence: The Art of Being at Home in Yourself*—is an accurate roadmap to the gifts that wait within. No one can drink there for you, but Tracy Cochran is a clear, wholehearted, and humble guide who helps us find our way home. So take this journey. It will help you live and introduce you to peace."

—MARK NEPO, author of *The Half-Life of Angels* and
Falling Down and Getting Up

"Every essay in this thoughtful and lyrical collection is a gem shining with deeply sensitive insights and reflections. From multiple angles, these essays show us how *presence*—close and clear attention to the realities of our lives—can open doors to wisdom and turn the humblest of events into revelations of beauty and goodness. Even danger and disappointment, Cochran demonstrates, can connect us to previously untouched dimensions of meaning."

—VEN. BHIKKHU BODHI, Buddhist scholar and translator

"*Presence* takes us on a delightful journey brimming with stories, wisdom, practices, and possibility. As Tracy Cochran draws from the well of her own life experience, she offers us a mirror into our own, inviting us to shed the myriad ways we create separateness and dropping open to the authentic experience of being human. Wonderfully wise, gently compassionate, *Presence* shines as a beacon in our troubled world."

—WENDY GARLING, author of *The Woman Who Raised the Buddha*

"I once got lost with Tracy in the woods. I was not afraid. We laughed a lot. We were closer to home than it seemed at the time. I had a similar sense of shared adventure reading *Presence*. I trusted her storytelling, her choosing careful, perfect words to take me to a new awareness—personal and startling."

—ANGELA DEWS, author of *Still, in the City*

PRESENCE

The Art of Being at Home in Yourself

TRACY COCHRAN

SHAMBHALA

Shambhala Publications, Inc.
2129 13th Street
Boulder, Colorado 80302
www.shambhala.com

Cover design: Linet Huamán Velásquez
Interior design: Kate E. White

9 8 7 6 5 4 3 2 1

First Edition
Printed in the United States of America

Shambhala Publications makes every effort
to print on acid-free, recycled paper.
Shambhala Publications is distributed worldwide by
Penguin Random House, Inc., and its subsidiaries.

LIBRARY OF CONGRESS CATALOGING-IN-PUBLICATION DATA
Names: Cochran, Tracy, author.
Title: Presence: the art of being at home in yourself / Tracy Cochran.
Description: Boulder: Shambhala Publications, 2024.
Identifiers: LCCN 2023023384 | ISBN 9781645471806 (trade paperback)
Subjects: LCSH: Consciousness—Religious aspects—Buddhism. | Self-
realization—Religious aspects. | Spiritual life—Buddhism—Miscellanea.
Classification: LCC BQ4570.P76 C63 2024 | DDC 294.3/444—dc23/
eng/20230823
LC record available at https://lccn.loc.gov/2023023384

For Alexandra

CONTENTS

PART THREE: *Mind*

PART FOUR: *The Whole Truth*

FOREWORD

"I am in a long-term committed relationship with life," Tracy Cochran writes in these pages. She gently dares us to do as much and shows on every page, in crystalline language, how to proceed. It's no use highlighting passages or putting Post-it tabs on exceptional places in the text—there would be too many. This book as a whole is an exceptional place.

It is a book for us all, doubters and believers, practitioners and wayward souls with an unquenched interest in living well. Its author is a teacher of Buddhist meditation in the New York region who has been nourished and informed by many Buddhist teachers and schools as well as the Gurdjieff Work. There used to be a question about what American Buddhism is: voices and meanings were still emerging even twenty years ago. The question strikes me as resolved now and in part resolved by American Buddhist women, who embody with grace, rigor, and modernity the ancient, ever-new teaching. Tracy Cochran is strongly individual as a writer and speaker and firmly placed in her tradition. That is a precious combination, needed by every teaching if it is to endure.

Lineage and genealogy are perennial concerns in Buddhism. Who taught whom, reaching back through the ages to the Awakened One himself. I vividly recall at a Zen temple the rhythmic recitation of lineage names reaching from the teacher present in the hall to innumerable ancestors. It's not so much about the names of persons largely unknown as about sustained transmission. Surprisingly, the cover design of this book offers a lineage clue through its adoption of a traditional Japanese motif called *maki-e*: a wave of fine gold powder that you might find as the background of a calligraphic scroll or on the lid of a lacquer box. *Maki-e* often brightens the scroll-mounted poetry of the most celebrated woman poet of nineteenth-century Japan, Otagaki Rengetsu, or Lotus Moon. There is such affinity between Tracy Cochran's mind and voice and Rengetsu's. They are both women of religion endowed with lyrical perceptiveness, love of life, untiring curiosity, and humor. Rengetsu was in later years a nun, a poet, a potter, a recluse who was always being found. Once, when the fall season was brightest, she confessed in a few lines of poetry that she could competently follow the precept of detachment—except just then, when the maple trees were so beautiful.

This is Rengetsu's problem—and Tracy Cochran's. The author of this book is a formidable storyteller, a hopeless lover of the gift of language, with a fate or karma that entangles her in amazing incidents and scrapes from which she barely escapes—with new knowledge and with confidence in the abiding presence in herself and in all human beings.

Some writers' autobiographies burden us with their achievements and dilemmas. Here, where she draws on life experience, Tracy Cochran allows us to see transparently through her life to our own: challenges, yes, and such promise through caring for awareness.

—ROGER LIPSEY

Presence

INTRODUCTION

In the middle of the journey of our life I found myself
in a dark wood where the straight way was lost.
—*DANTE*

In the middle of a journey across the country I found myself in a broken-down VW van on an empty highway in the Midwest. I still remember the death rattle of the engine and the shock of sudden stillness, of going somewhere and then suddenly not. I still recall how it felt to stand looking down a long, straight road under a burning blue sky, cornfields and prairie stretching as far as the eye could see. I remember how it felt to be in the middle of nowhere, which is what we call places we don't plan on landing in. I remember how it felt to have absolutely no clue what would happen next.

Years later, I remember that landscape as astonishingly beautiful, the bountiful American heartland. But at the time I saw a wilderness. It was the summer after college, and I was supposed to be traveling across the country with a stop in Boulder, Colorado. There

I hoped to meet a renowned lama and teacher of Tibetan Buddhist meditation. I meditated already, but I wanted to arrange to study with a master. This would be my graduate school, I decided: not books, but embodied experience.

Before the engine blew up, I didn't pay much attention to the land I was passing through. It was a blur in the background. It was time and distance away from my dream. I was picturing myself meditating under the gaze of a real Tibetan Buddhist lama in the foothills of the Rockies. I imagined him saying wise and insightful things, looking at me with wise and compassionate eyes. I pictured the kind of guru encounter I had read about in books. He would see deep inside me, past my doubts and resistance and all the weird little defensive moves of my ego. He would show me that there was an awareness in me that wasn't bound by any of that, a spacious awareness that was compassionate and free.

Instead, I stood stranded on the side of a road under an endless sky that didn't see or care about me. I remember feeling utterly exposed and very small. I felt as if I had startled awake from a dream. What was going to happen next? I had been rolling along with this story in my head and now this. The driver of the van, a friend from college, stood a few yards away, privately fuming. We agreed that we had a major situation on our hands, but we disagreed about who was to blame.

I blamed him. He argued that these kinds of things just happen out of a clear blue sky—as we stood there under a clear blue sky. I scolded him for not paying attention. But how connected to reality was I? I was furious and ashamed that I had heard ominous haunted house sounds coming out of the engine and thought nothing of it. Just like the land we were passing through, it was mere background. I was rolling along, spinning a fantasy about my life. I was imagining winning a spiritual golden ticket.

Instead, full stop. I stood there under the hot sun for what seemed like hours, having what seemed like the opposite of a spiritual experience. I was lost, not found. Unseen under the heavens. No cars. No clue what to do. Finally, a friendly driver in a pickup truck pulled over and drove us to a service station in town.

I was stranded for many days in Mendota, Illinois. Years later, I learned that *Mendota* is derived from a Native American word that means "junction of two trails." I think of it as the fork in the road.

"Your path is at your feet whether you realize it or not," the painter Agnes Martin once said in an interview.

It was during this time that a shift quietly took place inside me. It dawned on me that what I was seeking was not "out there," down the road, ahead in time and in better conditions. It is right here, right now, available to me, to all of us, just as we are. I knew that I needed teachings and guides, and over the years I found them. But starting with that experience of standing there in that seeming wilderness, I sensed the presence of something else—something beyond words, beyond all that people and our culture and the whole world can give us.

At first, the shift toward presence felt like giving up. I accepted the situation, but as the days passed, this acceptance softened and opened in an interesting way. I was more present—not just to others but to myself. *What am I doing here?* This question shifted from reproach—*how could I let this happen?*—to a kind of awe. *What am I doing here on earth? What are my true possibilities?*

While we waited for a new engine, the driver of the van and I befriended some of the young locals that hung out at a bar/café where we ate most meals. One night we were invited to drive around with them. One of the young men in the group had an old, lovingly maintained convertible. We cruised around with the top down—through the town and out into the countryside. I remember looking out across at the cornfields and prairie and up at the stars. I had thought I was in the middle of nowhere, but I was in the heart of the cosmos.

The young driver said that this is what they did most nights, drove around in circles because there was nowhere to go. This amazed me. There were no walls around the town. What was holding them back? How could they not see how awesome this place was? How could they not see that they were surrounded by a vast mystery? How could they not feel connected to it? How could I not see this and feel it?

This is a book about my search for answers to those questions. In the years to come, I would learn that the real meaning of mindfulness is presence. Along the way, there would be many adventures, many teachers in many traditions and no tradition. I would teach mindfulness meditation and mindful writing in museums, schools, corporations, and medical settings. But ultimately what I learned and taught and what I share here is about something beyond any teaching or label or formal practice. This is a book about the power of presence to bring us home to the wholeness and goodness of our lives.

> Be patient toward all that is unsolved in your heart and try
> to love the questions themselves, like locked rooms and like
> books that are now written in a very foreign tongue.
> —*RAINER MARIA RILKE*

The stories and practices offered here are meant to be entertainment and inspiration for your own gentle questioning. Asked what enlightenment is, a Zen master replied, "small moments many times." Be open to moments in your own life. Be patient and love the mystery and all the weird little twists life takes.

I've taken as my structure the Buddha's Four Foundations of Mindfulness: awareness of the body, of the feelings, of mind states or emotions, and of the deeper truths and realities that appear in times of greater clarity and presence. The Buddha offered these different ways of paying attention as a guide to meditation, specifically to monks in seclusion. But this book is for everyone, no matter what our conditions.

May this book inspire you to explore your own life with that spacious, kind awareness called presence. May it guide you to your own deepest truth.

INTRODUCTION TO THE PRACTICES

Attention is the rarest and purest form of generosity.
—*SIMONE WEIL*

Sati, the ancient Pali word for mindfulness, means to remember our experience in the present moment. Yet mindfulness might just as well be called "bodyfulness" or "heartfulness" because truly complete awareness of the present moment includes awareness of the body, the feelings, and the thoughts, as well as what is happening outside us. The term I use for this mindful, bodyful, heartful, open attention is *presence*.

It is helpful to choose a time to be present to our own experience. It can be in the morning, after work, or any instance we have a bit of ease. But it's important to remember that even one small moment is enough. I used to teach subway meditation to young New Yorkers, helping them claim time for themselves on the train between stops. This practice can be done sitting or standing. It can be done as a solitary exercise, combining mindfulness meditation with writing in a journal or on a computer. But it can also be practiced in a group, sitting together and sharing reflections from the exercises.

Working alone or together, the practice begins when we bring kind attention to our experience, allowing that experience to be just as it is. When we are present, our experience expands. The quality of the attention we bring in these moments is like being in the company of the most wonderful friend or guide or beloved. It is compassionate and curious, inviting us to relax and be open to be seen, trusting that everything is acceptable and worthy of exploration.

Traditional descriptions of mindfulness are wonderfully varied, but my favorite description has to be "absence of madness." It is a way of seeing that is unclouded. It is open sky awareness, characterized by a willingness to be present to what is, not deluded or resisting or running away. If you were sitting in a monastery, this quality of attention might be described as dispassionate or impartial, but in the thick of our lives this openness feels warm, like the sun coming out from behind the clouds. We long to be seen and heard and witnessed by a presence that knows us with acceptance and care.

Readers will discover that change comes not with grim will but with a willingness to engage with the world with acceptance and care. They will experience how presence can accompany them everywhere like a wise and compassionate friend. Presence can illuminate and transform even some of the darkest backstreets of our pasts. Scenes that make our hearts twist may soften; people who hurt us—or whom we hurt—may gain depth and dimension. Together we will discover that our own lives can be our path—not a poor substitute for a monastery but rather exactly the right conditions we need to heal and transform. The secret, as a Tibetan Buddhist lama once phrased it, is learning to turn toward presence as a trustworthy friend, willing to accompany us as we explore our lives in "short moments many times."

"Perhaps all the dragons of our lives are princesses waiting to see us act just once with courage," wrote Rilke in *Letters to a Young Poet*. "Perhaps every terror is, at its core, something helpless that wants our help."[1]

PART ONE

Body

Stories about the body and sensations ground and settle us. Drawing our attention to the felt experience of being alive also opens us to the sense of belonging to the greater world of creation. Coming home to the experience of being in a body—remembering the smell of snow or the sounds of the forest at night—loosens the grip of thought, reminding us that we are also part of a living world that is always fresh and always offering itself to us in surprising ways.

1

Down the Well

When I think of wellness, I can't help but think of my great-aunt Tilley who was trapped in an actual well for a good long while. This is not a play on words. We wish people well, but real wellness is deeply personal. It isn't the same as health, although these states are often paired. Well-being requires a deep encounter with our experience, and Tilley undoubtedly had that.

Tilley lived with my great-uncle Walter in a cabin in the Adirondacks lakes region. They lived a life of woodsy seclusion, simple and close to nature, although no one would have called Walter "contemplative." I have one childhood memory of him leaping around our living room, acting out the drama of a bear getting up on the roof of his cabin. Walter scared off the bear (which he pronounced "bar") by firing a shotgun into the air. Boom! No more bar!

"Quick, close the drapes," my mother said to me. She was from a very different kind of family, prosperous but reticent Danish immigrants, and she literally cringed at the prospect of the neighbors seeing Walter filling up the picture window, lunging and roaring like a bear.

My father's family were among the earliest European settlers in this country, and almost all of them ended up like Walter. They were farmers or sailing captains on the St. Lawrence River or skilled artisans—storybook kinds of callings, not modern professions. I asked my father why, and he said they didn't care for progress or commerce and, to their credit, they hated slavery, so they just kept living as their ancestors had, moving farther north and upriver and deeper into the woods.

"Let's face it, it takes a special talent to land here that early and stay that poor," said my father, roaring with laughter. I found the family strange and embarrassing until well into adulthood when I began to be intrigued by the way they flat out resisted a culture that stressed achievement and success in material terms above all. The farmers among them didn't even honor daylight savings time because "the cows didn't bother with it." They chose to live by the seasons and the river currents, finding stability and well-being in larger cycles.

I once read that First Nations Australians call modern Western people "line people" because we live our lives in a headlong forward march, as compared to their own sense of being part of a great circle of life. But Walter and his relatives were clearly not line people. And as commendable as this was in some ways, it had drawbacks—like the day Walter lowered his wife Tilley into the well and went off to town, leaving her there.

"Why on earth would he do that?" I asked my father.

"Well, they were repairing it or checking it, what else?" said my father. "They didn't live in a big city, did they?"

My father didn't understand why I wanted to live in New York City, a place where people wouldn't know how to maintain their own wells even if they had them. He called New Yorkers, including me, "cliff dwellers."

"But why did he go off and leave her?"

"He forgot she was down there, can you imagine?" My father laughed, seeing the humor in it, not the trauma, and assuring me that Walter rushed right back once he remembered.

And that was the whole story my father told. Walter went off to do errands in the nearest town and forgot that he had lowered poor Tilley into the well. I pictured Walter entering the general store in an Adirondack village and being greeted by the proprietor. Perhaps he was asked how he and Tilley were, and at the mention of her name, Walter suddenly realized that she wasn't just fine, thank you, but stuck in a well. He hurried home, reeled her up, and that was that.

Follow-up questions didn't shed much light. I was assured that the pair stayed together, although they never had children, which my father allowed was probably a good thing. Tilley was a sensitive woman with some issues, the daughter of a brilliant physics professor. How on earth was that improbable match made? And how was she after the well?

"If Tilley had issues when she went in, she had more coming out," a friend commented after I told this story to a small group. "Or else she was completely healed."

I like thinking that Tilley found healing in the depths, but I have no way of knowing. I do know that she was literally suspended in darkness, looking toward a light that was out of reach, possibly calling out for help from above that didn't come. At some point while she was dangling there it must have crossed her mind that she had made a huge mistake agreeing to go down that well, and maybe marrying Walter as well. But over the years I have come to understand that being suspended between doubt and faith, being utterly alone with your own experience and bereft of all hope of rescue from outside, is the wellspring of wellness.

Not many of us have volunteered to go down a dark well only to be abandoned there by an absent-minded partner. But most of us have received our very own boxes of darkness. We do know how it feels to be vulnerable and all alone. We know how it feels to be left hanging in the darkness of the unknown. And we know that although we are literally wired to avoid such situations, to fight and flee and freeze them out—they really are gifts.

We wish to be well, to overcome all obstacles and live with ease. But in the stillness of our hearts, we know that true wellness requires a deep dive into the well of our own experience. It requires that we be willing to be in the darkness and find the light that blooms in the midst of it. This light is not a metaphor or a distant possibility for a mystical few, but an attention that is right here, right now, as close as the body, able to see us as we really are without judgment, present with our pain and our limitations as well as our unexpected capacity for acceptance and strength.

It is in the dark times—those of no escape—we discover that it is not doing but awareness, and not striving but accepting, that heals and liberates. In the moments of deepest solitude we discover that we aren't alone but accompanied by this attention that watches without words, making more space around us.

There can be no doubt that Tilley must have felt that she had made a terrible mistake going down that well. It's easy to imagine her regret as she dangled there, calling out for Walter. She might well have reviewed quite a few mistakes and resolved to live very differently if only she did survive. But seeing ourselves as we really are, the way that we understand in times of no escape, brings the insight that much of what we do is mistaken. We react to life instead of consciously participating in it.

The great Japanese Zen sage Dogen taught that practice meant seeing ourselves making one mistake after another. Enlightenment expands awareness of this state of affairs. The life of a Zen master, according to Dogen, is one continuous mistake. This captures exactly how it feels to enter the present moment. We feel awkward and unbalanced and unprepared. Awareness exposes us, shining a light on our reactivity, our guardedness, our fears and desires and delusions.

When the chips are really down, as the expression goes, when all the exits are blocked and we are alone with ourselves, we feel how much of our energy is usually turned outward. The great paradox is that when we allow ourselves to be alone with our experience, not talking about it with others out loud or in our heads, when we resolve to let go and sink into the feeling beneath the words, we discover that feelings and fates are not fixed but fluid. We are more than we think we are, even in the darkest times.

Under the mind that is thinking and spinning stories, there is a deeper mind, an awareness that sees with acceptance. Under the heart that is broken and yearning, there is a deeper heart, bright and compassionate. We discover that we are not alone but accompanied by awareness, surrounded by love, even as we wait for rescue.

How I came to know about Great-Uncle Walter and Great-Aunt Tilley is part of the lesson I learned about wellness. My father told me that near the St. Regis Mohawk Reservation in the Adirondack lakes region of northern New York, he met an aspiring artist from New York City. This young man was traveling all around this remote region, exploring the life and people he encountered. My father was impressed by this young artist's interest, so different from that of the hippies who ventured north to start communes. My father and I spoke to a group of them once who told us that living close to the land would be a piece of cake compared to the pressures of the big city.

"They won't last long," my father told me of the hippies. "The minute winter comes, they'll be gone."

Respect nature, this was part of the lesson. Learn about where you are. Winter is harsh in the North Country. And also respect the people who live in a place. Be curious, investigate, learn from them. Don't assume you know more than they do or treat the world like it's yours for the taking. The young artist showed my father his sketch-book, full of studies of nature and animals and people. My father flipped through it, admiring forest scenes, young and old faces, white and Mohawk, and then one image brought him to a full stop.

"What an amazing character he was," said the New York artist. "That man lived in a log cabin deep in the woods. He wore a World War I helmet and carried a shotgun and didn't tell stories so much as act them out."

"By God, if it wasn't my Uncle Walter," said my father.

Learn about your relatives and your ancestors—this was the other part of the lesson. Don't assume that you have grown beyond them. And also remember that the first and wisest people on this land regarded everything around them, not just humans related by blood but also plants and animals and the earth and stars, as relatives and ancestors. Wellness, they understood, depends on knowing our place in a greater cycle.

"Today we have gathered and see that the cycles of life continue." The Mohawk people gave (and still give) thanks together often. They offer thanks to the People, to Mother Earth and all her plants and herbs and creatures, to the Sun, the Moon, the Stars, the Waters, the Four Winds, and the Teachers.[2]

The word *Mohawk* was all around me growing up in northern New York: Mohawk River, Mohawk Valley, the Niagara Mohawk Power Company. I was surrounded by reminders of a nation vanquished by my European ancestors, the colonizing settlers who ultimately gave rise to Great-Uncle Walter and me.

The People of the Flint, the Keepers of the Eastern Door, the most easterly of six nations of the Haudenosaunee, the great Iroquois Confederacy, the Mohawk, along with all the other Indigenous people, practiced and still practice gratitude as a way of life. They understood and still understand that we belong to creation and to each other. No matter what happened to them at the hands of the European settlers, my ancestors—and what happened was unspeakable—they understood that gratitude and that knowing and naming their relatives and their place in great nature was the way to wellness, to a greater wholeness.

"We have been given the duty to live in balance and harmony with each other and all living beings. So now, we bring our minds together as one as we give greetings and thanks to each other as People."

The millions of Indigenous people who inhabited this land lived in a state of such harmony and balance that the European colonists who first landed here thought very few people were about. It was like walking into a pristine home and concluding that it had to be empty because otherwise it would be a mess.

The Mohawk Thanksgiving Greeting ends with giving thanks for the Creator, or Great Spirit, the animating force in everything, the source of "all the love that is still around us." Even when everything was lost to them, they gave thanks for a love that can never be taken.

These were the people the European settlers called "savages." It would not be wrong to read our entire colonial history as one continuous mistake, ranging from crimes against humanity and the earth to our smaller daily mistakes of distraction and omission, on the scale of Walter leaving Tilley in the well. How can we even begin to atone? By remembering that the root meaning of *atone* is "at one." By remembering that we are not independent but interdependent, and that our wellness inside and out depends upon realizing that we are part of a greater whole.

Awakening means opening our hearts to the whole of our experience, including our own darkness and pain. It is a relief to know that we can start small, sitting quietly at a quiet time of day or in a quiet place. We can practice saying "forgiven" like a mantra or prayer when difficult feelings or memories arise. This might feel presumptuous. Who am I to forgive myself? But it is really a practice of coming out of hiding, of viewing ourselves in a new light. We can practice this way when any kind of difficult feeling comes up: a memory, a rush of anxiety, that uneasy sense that we are puppets dancing on the strings of our conditioning. For a moment or two we can allow all that to emerge into the light of a more spacious presence.

Throughout the ages, people have called this greater presence God. But we don't need to worry about whether or not there is a God and if God forgives us. We just need to practice accepting our own humanity. One moment at a time, we can practice opening to our life—just that. This act of opening does not depend on belief or views of any kind. It depends on being still, as Dogen taught. It depends on sinking into the well of our experience, opening to what arises, excluding nothing.

As we learn to open to accept our own rage and grasping and pain, we also discover that we are opening to a greater presence. Moment by moment, we realize that this isn't something far away, but as close as knowing that you are reading these words.

One of the passengers on the *Mayflower* was my tenth great-grandfather, a young man notable mainly for the good fortune of surviving. He made the spectacular mistake of coming up on deck for fresh air during a brutal storm and washed overboard. He grabbed a rope and hung on, living to have ten children and eighty grandchildren and ultimately two million descendants. What if all of them, or even one in two million, sat down and opened to the true scale of the gift of being alive, realizing that every other living being is a relative?

The root of the word *forgive* means "to give or grant or allow." Forgiveness begins with a willingness to be seen, not by your thinking mind but by an awareness that represents a greater wholeness.

What can we learn from the Mohawk and all the First Peoples who lived on this continent? Even in the face of the greatest darkness, we can drop into the sensation and feeling of being alive, noticing and giving thanks for this and for an attention that embraces what it finds, holding everything, no matter how dark, with acceptance and love.

We awaken to the whole of our lives, past, present, and future. The root of *heal* is "to make whole." During the long dark night that preceded his awakening, the Buddha reached down and touched the earth. Like the Mohawk, like Dogen, and even possibly like poor Tilley, the Buddha understood that we don't dwell in separation. Our whole being seeks to wake up, not our thinking minds alone. The plants and animals and other people in the world are not just obstacles or decorations. They are meant to touch our hearts and our senses and our deepest feelings, nurturing and guiding us toward what is truly valuable and real.

Here is a last line from the Mohawk thanks to the Creator: "Everything we need to live a good life is here on Mother Earth." This does not mean there is no trouble or suffering, no injustice, no despair. It does not mean that we don't have a great deal of work to do. It means that no matter how dark our lives are, we are not alone. Life is with us. Presence is with us. We have what we need to be well.

"Be islands unto yourselves, refuges unto yourselves. . . ." As he lay dying, the Buddha gave this advice to his beloved disciple Ananda, who was imploring his great teacher for guidance for himself and his fellow monks. Some versions of this teaching use the word *lamp*. The word *dīpa* means both "island" and "lamp." *Island* is the accepted meaning, but the essential sense is the same.

The Buddha spoke of being your own refuge. He didn't mean be cut off from the rest of life. Meditating means unplugging from the thinking mind that endlessly compares ourselves to others. It means turning the attention to our own experience, accepting it as it is so that we might directly experience the cause of sorrow. Even in a life of total seclusion, alone in a cave or a cell or on an actual island, a person couldn't help but notice the life inside and outside changing, waxing and waning.

Be your own laboratory, your own living proof. See that this is the nature of life. See that the truth of suffering does not separate you from others; it unites you. The Buddha didn't mean be totally self-sufficient, proudly independent above all, beholden to no one. The Buddha along with all wise beings understood that our freedom and our power comes as we start to realize that we are part of a greater whole, and that we owe thanks in every direction for this life of ours, inside and outside, up and down, north, south, east, and west, the way Native people give thanks.

By being an island the Buddha meant be grounded, dare to touch the earth of your own living experience in the present moment, not grasping for ideas from outside, from "experts," but being willing to experience the living truth. The practice of meditation allows us to settle down and open up. As we learn to relax, we travel from the surface to the depths of our human experience. We might feel, for example, how good it is to be alive, and how mysterious. Last night was despair, perhaps, and yet here we are, supported by benevolent forces.

We may realize the true scale of the present. It contains the whole of our lives. In such a moment it can seem as if our ancestors are with us, witnessing life through our eyes. Or we can discover that our sense of isolation is an illusion. We can suddenly realize that we are not to blame for all the ills of the world—and become free to truly respond. Beneath all that thinking, those defensive postures, that delusion that clouds the mind, we are responsive creatures. We are kinder than we think. We are more.

The Buddha taught that craving is the root of all suffering. Another way to understand being an island is being still in the midst of that flood of desire and grasping while observing and experiencing craving without reacting. Scientific research shows that mindfulness quiets the part of the mind involved in rumination and obsession.

As we learn to be still, we let go of stories about who we are that are based on not having what we want and being burdened with what we don't want.

Being an island means remembering where we are and who we are, that we are living beings on a living earth, under a sun, part of a vast and mysterious web of life. In such moments we see that attention itself is an extraordinary gift and a means of transformation and freedom. As an experiment, notice how it feels to stop and be still in the midst of the rushing stream of life. Allow yourself to remember to the depth and extent of your life. If you wish, tell about it.

2

The Night I Died

Head down, hugging a grocery bag, I hurried past gutted buildings and empty lots, back to my ex-boyfriend's apartment in Hell's Kitchen. It seemed like a good idea at some point, having dinner together as friends. But the little Spanish market on the corner of Ninth Avenue and West 35th Street was the only pocket of light and warmth for blocks. Ahead there was nothing but deserted streets and a cold wind blasting in from the dark Hudson River.

I wondered what I was doing in this godforsaken place, when exactly I had become so insubstantial, agreeing to go out to the store alone at ten, agreeing to do all kinds of things I didn't really want to do. I shivered a little with self-pity.

Manhattan in the 1980s was a gritty place. I used to think of it as having a dark glamour but no more. A few years before, I had come to Manhattan like someone drawing close to a fire. I wanted to be warmed, enlightened. But nothing turned out the way I had hoped, not love, not work, not life. I pictured myself a waif huddling along in a bleak neighborhood, bringing her own pasta to dinner.

The image was so pathetic that I savored it, a fragment of a modern Dickens tale.

I was passing an empty parking lot on West 35th Street near Tenth Avenue when three men rushed out at me from the shadows of a gutted tenement across the street. I heard them before I saw them, pounding toward me, whipping past me, stopping and wheeling around, taking up stations around me, as purposeful and practiced as football players—or predators.

For a few moments, we stood and stared at each other. Incredibly, I was gripped by an impulse to smile and make eye contact, to defuse the situation by establishing that we were all fellow human beings, even potentially friends. They were not interested in making friends.

They were pumped up, panting, panicking. Two looked like lanky teenagers, wraithlike in dark hooded sweatshirts, eyes glazed with fear. The third was older and much bigger. A faded green sweatshirt stretched taut across his chest. His wrists dangled out of the sleeves, as if he were wearing someone else's clothes—and maybe he was, because the next day there were reports in the papers of escaped convicts in the area. His broad face was grim.

Darting behind me, he jerked his arm tight across my throat. I felt his chest heave and heard the rasping of his breath. Staring up at the side of his face, I saw a long shiny scar. It was strange to be pulled so close to someone intent on harming me, but even stranger was the sudden pang of compassion I felt for him, for the wounding that had made the scar, for the suffering he must feel to be doing this.

It was the strangest thing. Brain studies show that the readiness of the body to move precedes our awareness of being willing and intending to move, that everything that happens is dependent on thousands—millions—of conditions and turnings of little wheels that take place below our ordinary limited level of consciousness. But the burst of compassion I felt didn't seem like an unconsciously conditioned response, like the impulse to smile at my muggers—like almost everything I found myself doing. It was as if another, higher consciousness were descending into my consciousness.

I once read a story about how no animals were found among the dead after a tsunami; sensing the infinitesimal vibration of what was coming, they headed for higher ground. Even before I could grasp what was happening to me there in the street, it was as if the animal of my body and my physical brain were heading for higher ground, opening to receive help from above. Even before I glimpsed the light, my heart was opening to a kind of feeling that cannot be created or destroyed by anyone, only received.

"Money!" His voice was a rasp. His massive arm was pressing down on nerves that made it impossible for me to move my arm to reach the money in my front pocket, and I couldn't talk to tell him this. "Money now!" He pulled his grip tighter. My vision started going black around the edges. I remember thinking the situation was absurd. I couldn't talk. I couldn't tell him that I needed to be released to get to my money.

But I also glimpsed the larger absurdity of the larger situation: I was a young woman alone at night on a deserted side street in Hell's Kitchen, drifting along thinking about what she liked and didn't like about her life, what she judged to be good and bad, dreaming that she was in control of what happened, all the while oblivious to reality. "When a man knows he is to be hanged in a fortnight, it concentrates his mind wonderfully,"[3] observed Samuel Johnson. My mind suddenly terribly concentrated, I saw I was in real trouble.

My brain started working faster than it had ever worked, calculating the size and strength of my attacker, the agility of the two young men guarding me, my own capacities, and the probability of this or that happening if I did this or that. My brain calculated and recalculated every aspect of the situation I was in until it concluded there could be no escape, no movie-like scene of flipping my attacker with deadly martial arts skills, throwing him into his assistants and running away. The reality I confronted was inconceivable, unworkable. My brain crashed; the screen went white. I surrendered.

It was then that I saw the light, just a glow at first but growing brighter until it became dazzling, welling up in the darkness to fill my whole body and mind. As it grew, this light gained a force and direction—an authority unknown to me. I remember marveling at the building intensity and intention, wondering where it had come from, not just low down in my body but from unseen depths—and then it became a column of brilliant white light that shot out of the top of my head, arcing high into the night sky.

A Tibetan Buddhist I met who had read an earlier account of what happened to me that night told me it reminded her of a Vajrayana Buddhist practice called *phowa*. I also learned that *Vajrayana* means "diamond" or "thunderbolt" vehicle, which I understood personally because everything about my experience dazzled, was charged with force. Phowa is described as a practice of conscious dying, or transference of consciousness at the time of death, or even a flash of enlightenment without meditation. Tibetan lamas imprisoned by the Chinese were said to be able to leave their bodies this way.

But this—happening to someone who could barely sit still for a twenty-minute meditation—didn't amaze me as much as what unfolded next. The column of light joined a much greater light that descended to meet it. Behind the abandoned tenements, behind my attackers, behind all the appearances in this world, there was a gorgeous luminosity. It was clear to me that this light was the force that holds up the world, into which all separation dissolves.

I realized that I could see myself and my attacker from behind and above. I watched myself gasping, watched my knees buckling, watched myself sink, watched myself looking up at the light. And then I was embraced by the light.

Science argues that while near-death experiences feel real, they are simply fantasies or hallucinations caused by a brain under severe stress, and certainly my brain was under stress that night. A choke hold can kill in twenty to thirty seconds. Someone skilled in martial arts can knock someone out within eight seconds using such a hold, and brain damage can happen after about fifteen seconds because stopping blood flow to and from the brain can lead to brain hemorrhage and the pressure on the heart can cause it to stop.

But science can't account for the intimacy—for the extraordinary presence—of the experience. I didn't just *see* the light; I was *seen* by it—and not in part but in whole. I knelt on the sidewalk, looking up at a light that was not separate from wisdom and love, a light that descended to meet me.

Afterward, I heard the phrases "communion of saints," "heavenly host," and "vault of heaven" and felt a thrill of recognition—my mind grasped at religious metaphors to describe what I had experienced. The light was vast, vaulted, and all around. I sensed the presence of beings, ranks of beings, an ascending multitude, turning, moving, altogether forming a great witnessing consciousness, in every detail and part infinitely finer and higher than my own. There are no words for the majesty and radiance of what I glimpsed and how it made me feel—lifted, seen, accepted into a vast whole.

A particular being drew very close, looking down at me from above with love that had a gravity and grace unlike anything I had ever known. It proceeded to search me, brushing aside everything I thought I knew about myself—my name, my education, all my labels—as if it were not just unimportant but unreal. I once came up with an awkward personal metaphor for the urgency of this part of my experience: firefighters searching a burning building, shining a light through the smoke, looking for signs of life while there was still time. Strangely, I sensed that the urgency and concern weren't for my physical life.

Finally, the searching stopped. The light came to rest at a particular spot in the center of my chest. It poured through me. I was very
still, in thrall, humbled, aware that what was dear and good to this
light was not any quality that I knew, but something deep and mute
in my being. How long was I held in the grave and loving gaze of this
higher being, this angel of awareness? Moments probably, but time
meant nothing. I had the sensation that my whole life—lived and as
yet unlived—was spread out for examination, that my life was being
read like a book, weighed like a stone in the palm of a hand.

I saw that everything counted—or, everything real, every tear,
all our suffering. That I didn't "believe" in any of this—that I was
too cool, too skeptical, too educated to be dazzled by experiences
that were clearly, had to be, subjective, that I would never resort
to hackneyed religious metaphors, and images like weighing and
reading--also didn't count. My opinions about what I believed or
didn't believe, what I was capable of or not capable of, were just
smoke to be brushed away.

I was lifted up into a field of light and love, flooded with a feeling
of liberation, of rejoicing. It was like flying, rising above the clouds
into bright sunlight, except that it was more radiant. It was exalted,
sublime yet welcoming. Everything I knew fell away, yet I felt completely accepted and acceptable, completely known, completely
loved, completely free. There were no words, just experience. Yet ever
since, I have wondered if this is what salvation is like, to be lifted up
out of the fog of separation, of sin, of forever missing the mark, and
delivered into the whole, into the reality behind the appearances of
the world.

It was clear that this radiant light, this loving consciousness,
held everything that is. It was the alpha and omega, the particle and
wave, the unifying force of the universe, suffusing us, carrying us
when we leave this body, accompanying us always and everywhere,
appearing in us when we are open to receive.

I knew I wouldn't stay long in this radiance, in this sublime love and freedom. I was still sinking to my knees on a dirty sidewalk in Hell's Kitchen, still struggling to breathe. Yet, as strange as it sounds, I wasn't struggling inside. I was still. It felt as if I were falling to my knees in prayer—surrendering, not to this attack but to something that was infinitely higher. I understood that a life could have a different sense and meaning, that it could be spent seeking, purifying, practicing—I couldn't find a word to convey the glimpse I had better than the words of the prayer: "Thy Kingdom come, Thy Will be done, on Earth as it is in Heaven."

The being who searched me—who saw me inside and outside, past, present, and future—told me without words to relax, the struggle would soon pass, I would not be harmed. I would return. I would go on. The light withdrew.

My attacker loosened his grip just enough to allow me to reach a ten-dollar bill in the front pocket of my jeans. I threw the bill on the ground. My attacker jerked his arm off my throat, scooped up the bill, and ran off with the others. I stood up. I had my life back. I stared up at the night sky, then down at the ripped grocery bag, wondering why the muggers hadn't taken the cigarettes and the six-pack of beer.

I walked back to my ex-boyfriend's apartment, shaking with sobs. I hadn't been harmed. Settled at the long dining room table in his book-lined loft, tears streaming, I choked out the story, insisting that I wasn't harmed. Never mind the weeping, I told him. I was fine, really, perfectly calm at center of the storm, you see. My ex-boyfriend looked miserable. The crying went on and on. He pushed a twenty-dollar bill across the table toward me, repaying me for the groceries. I brushed it away, and he pushed it back. "Just take it."

We aren't in control in the way we think we are, I told him. Things happen, even terrible things, but they are not what they seem to be. And we aren't alone. There is a light, a luminosity behind the appearances of this world. There is a luminous, loving intelligence above us, watching over us, caring for us. I knew how this sounded. Religious, mystical, unbelievable. "Do you believe me, not about the mugging but about the light?" He shook his head no, scowling softly, sorry for me. He just could not.

In the weeks and years that followed, I learned this is how it goes with personal revelation. I was an unreliable narrator, no more so than any other ordinary human, but still very limited, subject to dreams, to the wheels and levers of conditioning. But the experience never grew dim. I told it to people I trusted or the dying. I told it to my father in his last days and to another dear old friend near his end. "I sure hope you're right," he said.

What we really have to share is not any spiritual treasure we imagine we have stored up, but our poverty, our common human situation, our inability to know.

Many years after that night in Hell's Kitchen, I still drift through the world lost in thought, captivated by stories and images. But I know a greater reality and a greater awareness exists. I know there is a truth that cannot be thought, only received.

"After great pain, a formal feeling comes," writes Emily Dickinson. "The Nerves sit ceremonious, like Tombs."[4]

After a great shock, a stillness comes. We may be very busy outside, but inside we are still. The world we knew and the narrative we constructed about our future have been blasted away. We may be able to go about our days, but inside we are in a state of suspension. We are grieving, sad, and afraid. It is best to "sit ceremonious" inside, just being. At such times, it is enough to be quiet and kind, to give ourselves the loving attention we would give a dear friend. This kind allowing, this not doing, not striving to fix or to know, allows us to touch the earth of our experience. You may feel completely lost in the world. But deep within, a new understanding may be taking root.

Understand comes from an Old English root that means "to stand in the midst of"—not under as you might think but in between or within something. There is a knowledge that comes from familiarity, from being with, the way a sailor understands the sea or the way you come to understand a friend. To comprehend this way is not a matter of words, but a feeling of recognition and remembrance of the good. Sitting helpless by a window, we may suddenly remember the warmth of the sun coming through feels good. A cup of tea is also good, and a moment when we remember to soften inside, to open to receive.

There are times in life when we feel lost, unmoored, wandering in a desert. These are the times that reveal the power of the smallest actions: inner movements of availability, a willingness to be with our experience with an attitude of acceptance and self-compassion, trusting that as we do this a deeper understanding will come.

3

We're in It Now

"I was looking right at the White House," my father said. "Can you imagine being right there when you heard that?"

My father always remembered driving down Pennsylvania Avenue in Washington, D.C., when President Roosevelt came on the radio to declare the day before, December 7, 1941, "a date which will live in infamy." People tend to remember exactly where they were and what they were doing when shocking news comes.

During that famous live broadcast, the president was not actually at the White House but in the nearby Capitol addressing a special joint session of Congress, asking for a declaration of war. The day before, the Empire of Japan had attacked U.S. military bases in Pearl Harbor, Hawaii, and declared war on the United States and Great Britain.

"I regret to tell you that very many American lives have been lost," said the president, calling my father and everyone in the country to arms.

I picture my father driving along Pennsylvania Avenue, his head full of thoughts and plans. Just months before, he had moved to

Washington, D.C., uprooting his life in northern New York, breaking with his mother's wishes in order to take a job working on the construction of the Pentagon. I imagine his excitement and anticipation, a young man from the rural North Country now living in a city preparing for war. The atmosphere everywhere would have been bustling and expectant. Everything was new. He would have been thinking about what he had to do, about difficulties and challenges large and small. And then FDR came on the radio, and my father's private world of thought would have evaporated like mist.

"We're in it now," my mother's father said at a dinner table in western Nebraska.

Moments of shock awaken us to a truth that we rarely glimpse in ordinary times: we are not separate and autonomous creatures, in control of a good portion of our lives.

My father, who was to meet and fall in love with my mother in the course of the war, shared that same observation, and so did most of the country. The live broadcast, which lasted about six minutes, was heard by the vast majority of Americans, and most of those listening remembered it in the indelible way my father did, when suddenly everybody stopped "going about their business." Everybody said or heard or thought to themselves: We're in it now.

It was as if the president had yelled, "Fire!" The response was immediate and overwhelming. Within the hour, Congress voted to declare war on Japan. The anti-war and isolationist movement collapsed on the spot.

Recruiting stations went on twenty-four hour duty to deal with the flood of volunteers seeking to enlist to serve, including my father. On December 11, 1941, Germany declared war on the United States, and we answered with our own declaration. Everyone who was qualified—and many who were not—dropped everything and ran to be one more pair of hands on the bucket brigade.

Virginia Woolf called the special memories that come in the midst of shock "moments of being," noting in her journals that she spent most of her waking hours with her head full of "cotton wool." But sometimes shocks came that woke her up from this dreamy state, igniting the sense that we are all part of a larger pattern.

Moments of shock awaken us to truths that we rarely glimpse in ordinary times: We are not separate and autonomous creatures, in control of a good portion of our lives. We are part of a greater living whole, inextricably connected to others and to the life around us. We are not as free as we think we are. We are subject to myriad conditions, but we are also capable of more than we think. We are living participants in a greater creation, vessels for greater energies and forces. We can choose what we serve.

"It did not really matter what we expected from life, but rather what life expected from us," wrote Austrian psychiatrist Viktor Frankl in *Man's Search for Meaning*, chronicling his time in a Nazi concentration camp during the war. "We needed to stop asking about the meaning of life and instead to think of ourselves as those who were being questioned by life—daily and hourly." [5]

Some seventy-five million people died in World War II but remarkably few Americans—405,399. Countless more people were wounded, orphaned, and displaced. My father was not among them. Like other American enlisted men, he went through three months of training and boarded a ship, willing to face whatever awaited him. The young men slept in hammocks on board and ate two meals a day, waiting and wondering what would come. It is astonishing to consider how little most of them knew when they were sent off to fight.

"They were always happy to have farm boys in a platoon because we knew how to do things," my father told me. He had spent summers on his grandfather's farm. "We knew how to chop wood and build fires and tell which way the wind was blowing." At least a few of them knew how to shoot.

For security purposes, none of the soldiers were told where they were bound until they were well out to sea. My father's ship headed toward the Pacific but he ended up in Panama, tasked with helping guard the Panama Canal against possible Japanese attack. Aside from sitting up all night in the jungle guarding a plane that had crashed from wild animals and would-be scavengers, he didn't see any action. He didn't have to kill or face the horror of war.

"I was ready to go wherever they sent me," he added when asked about his wartime experience, ever aware that he had been spared.

And yet he didn't emerge from the war unscathed. Certain shocks take a long time to do their work, slowly opening us and planting seeds. I once heard that the great martial artist Bruce Lee described certain blows that sent vibrations through the body that took years to bring a person down. At the end of his life, my father told me that in the middle of the jungle in Panama, he received a seemingly small shock that sent out ripples that changed his view of life and what really matters.

He met another soldier whom he knew from home. It's always startling to run into parts of our past when we are far away, although travel—and all the more so the dislocation of war—is renowned for providing fresh impressions of ourselves, heightened in new surroundings, exposing our assumptions and beliefs and ways and showing us how we are limited and how we might change.

In the midst of reminiscing about the North Country, this other young man happened to mention to my father how my father's own grandfather, the farmer with whom he spent summers, came to be called "One-Potato Cade."

"Do you know why people called him that?" my father asked me. A few possibilities popped into my mind but I refused to venture a guess.

Cade's hired man was invited to dinner, the story went. He was hungry from a long day working in the fields and, after eating a potato, went to help himself to a second one. But old Cade batted his hand away.

"One potato's enough for you," my father intoned, imitating Cade's proud, stern voice. "Can you imagine that?"

I couldn't, but my father looked at me with such sadness and disgust that I tried to soften the blow.

On the scale of sins someone can commit, I told him, denying a man a second potato has to rate pretty low. But my father shook his head.

"The real shame of it is that he grew potatoes."

My great-grandfather had no shortage of potatoes. He raised pigs and potatoes, the things he truly liked to eat.

And the worst of it, according to my father, wasn't just that outer act of meanness but the breaking of a deeper law: Any good farmer, any good person, my father told me, understands that kindness and generosity matter. The way you treat your neighbors and family, the way you treat everyone, matters. The hired man stood up from the table, collected his pitchfork, and left without looking back. Word got around.

"I always remembered that story," my father said. "I vowed that I wasn't going to be like that." My father could see that I knew that he hadn't always lived as if this were so.

There are seeds that need fire to sprout. The lodgepole pine and other trees have cones or fruits that are completely sealed with resin and can open to release their seeds only after the heat of a fire has melted the resin. Moments that spark shame or remorse can burn like cold fire. But if we can bear the suffering without fighting, freezing, fleeing, or fixing, if we can open to the experience and examine it with curiosity and acceptance, new seeds of understanding can be planted. These seeds can take a long time to grow.

I picture my father as a young soldier guarding the crashed plane in the jungle, an experience he vividly remembered. He had to keep watch all night. I imagine him sitting up, aware of the sounds outside and the sensations he had to be feeling inside, attuned to his heartbeat and his breathing. We innately return to the breath when we are alone in nature at night. We can't help but be aware that we are held in a mysterious web of life, surrounded by other beings and energies. His thoughts would have been still—the stillness that comes with vigilance.

He would have been afraid of what might come out of the darkness of this unknown place, a heightened version of the fear that arises in all of us that we are not enough to face what might come—that we are not brave enough or strong enough or smart enough, that we will be overwhelmed or devoured. And after that other young soldier told him that story, my father also had that extra twist of family shame that so many of us carry. Whether it is the secret knowledge of meanness or depression or addiction or abuse, we hold the shame close, hoping no one will discover what marks us as defective or lacking. But my father couldn't leave his post, so I choose to picture him as a spiritual warrior, quietly facing his life. He would have daydreamed and planned to pass the time, but at other moments he would have contemplated One-Potato Cade, still feeling pain and shame but also catching a glimpse of his true possibilities. He was more than the stories he carried.

Shocks burn. They make impressions that literally scar us. Yet, as we learn to be curious about these impressions, examining them with an attention that doesn't judge, we discover deeper feelings and truths. Slowly and gently, over a long time, we find that we are more than the stories we receive and tell ourselves. We discover that shame is the painful coating around tenderness and responsiveness. We remember that we have good hearts and minds, willing to open to give and receive.

I picture my great-grandfather Cade's farm on Pillar Point, a peninsula of land jutting into Lake Ontario. I remember how long and hard the winters were in my childhood. The lake ice was so thick you could drive a car on it. The soil was so rocky that in the old days the farmers had horses draw sleds called stoneboats through the fields to collect the stones, which were lined up and piled up to make boundary fences. When I see stone fences, I think of how hard their lives were, but also of how they contributed to their suffering with their grasping and fear.

I think of my father sitting in the jungle contemplating Cade and all his ancestors, settlers who treated the land like a dangerous wilderness to be subdued. I imagine my father questioning some of the values he was raised with surrounding the self-sufficient rugged individual, thrifty and industrious, beholden to no one.

I picture my father's heart and mind slowly opening like a closed fist. This took longer than one night in the jungle. By the end of his time in the military, my father was an officer. But by the end of his life, he was a kind and generous man.

"We're too old to cry over things," both my parents said to me when their house was destroyed in a hurricane. "It's relationships that matter. Love matters. Nothing else lasts."

During a visit I had with him months before he died, my father insisted on cooking a dinner for my sister and me—nothing fancy, meatloaf and baked potatoes (of course!). But he was well into his nineties, legally blind, and tethered to an oxygen tank due to emphysema and COPD, so he stopped to rest every fifteen minutes or so. I asked him if I could take over. He refused to let me.

"Do you want to know the secret of life?" my father asked. "You keep going for what you love, keep doing things for people you love. Just let things take as long as they take."

At the end of my father's funeral, because he was a military veteran, a rifle team of seven service members fired three volleys or rounds into the air. This was not, in spite of the twenty-one shots, an official 21-gun salute, which is reserved for heads of state. It was a military gun salute honoring an ordinary man who served.

According to military sources, the ritual of firing three volleys harkens back to ancient European wars, when fighting was halted to remove the dead and wounded from the field. The three rounds of shots signaled that the dead were cleared and properly cared for so the battle could resume.

Official military sources acknowledge that while the choice of seven rifles and three rounds may have biblical and mystical significance, the discharge of weapons, rendering them harmless, is universal. A military website points out that a North African tribe trailed the points of its spears on the ground to show that its warriors came in peace.

We have it in us to stop the battle. Some shocks teach us to drop into the depths of our hearts and minds, discovering that our true strength comes as we learn to open them rather than shutting down and armoring. Moment by moment, we learn what the first inhabitants of this land knew and what the oldest people know: We are part of life, not separate. Our own lives are brief and very limited, but we dwell in a great web of generosity. Consciously or unconsciously, we are constantly giving and receiving: breathing air, taking in food and impressions, offering our actions and words and presence. Life is constantly being offered to us while we are here, and we can't help but respond in myriad ways. Opening to this truth, we can choose what we give. We can give love.

Do you ever notice how it feels to do nothing? It can be interesting to set aside a certain period of time to shift your attention to the experience of being present. This does not need to be a formal meditation; you can keep your eyes open, but allow your gaze and your whole attitude to be soft and open. Notice the gaps between thought. Notice that you feel more deeply yourself, more deeply alive and present, in those moments when you are not thinking, just aware. Our deepest insights often come from this state of presence. Notice that we feel the most deeply ourselves and the most deeply alive and connected to life when we are *not* thinking.

How deeply we fear being nobody. One way to think of the ego is as a defense against pain, particularly the pain of being no one. It shores us up, reminding us that we are somebody. We update our internal résumés and narratives constantly. We seek new skills and go on self-improvement regimes of all kinds, including the practice of mindfulness meditation. And we may improve a little. We may feel a little more peaceful, a little more resilient and less quick to anger. This is good—and for many people good enough.

Yet deep down we may sense that even in the name of spiritual practice we are seeking to plant a flag in ground that gives way under our feet. Nothing we do can stop time's passage and all the things that keep happening that we don't want, like aging and loss. Even with a very deep and well-established practice that has grown new neurons and reduced stress and accomplished everything else that scientific studies promise, even then we still touch the sadness of life. We touch darkness and pain—and that fear of being no one.

It may come as a relief that in ancient times, when people first heard the Buddha's teachings on emptiness or no self, it was considered most auspicious to feel not joy but terror. One classic explanation is that to feel fear is to intuit what must come. The ego must volunteer to abdicate the throne in the center of your life. We must leave the skull-sized kingdom of our thinking and be no one, just presence, at least some of the time. We may begin a mindfulness practice just hoping for a little more peace or inner spaciousness, a better brain, and so on. But slowly, slowly the practice leads us to the realization that real peace and freedom come in those moments when we are present. We discover that being no one, or no one in particular, is not a diminishment but a deepening and expansion. It awakens us to our deep human nature, our shared nature, noticing that it isn't frozen but instead flows.

Presence is in all of us, but we forget. We yearn and strive to have a feeling of being alive, to create, to serve, to travel the world and explore ourselves. We forget that the way to a larger life is to stop doing, including the form of doing called thinking. Allow yourself to sit still and remember. The body knows the way. In times of hurt or sorrow, in the depths of winter, we naturally seek our own "Fortress of Solitude," as Superman called his polar retreat.

Allow the body to be soft and still. Let go of thinking. Notice that this doesn't separate us from life. It opens our awareness and shows us what is needed.

Our culture leads us to believe that we must *strive* to think and do in ever better and bigger ways. Superman, Batman, Spider-Man— all our quintessential comic book heroes—swoop in to perform astonishing deeds at crucial moments, but they also retreat into being nonheroes, becoming Clark Kent, a mild-manner reporter at the *Daily Planet*; the reclusive philanthropist Bruce Wayne; or Peter Parker, a high school student living in Queens, who anguishes about common teenage themes of rejection, loneliness, and belonging. As heroes these characters dazzle with their superhuman strength or resourcefulness and agility. Yet none of them do these deeds unmasked. As an exercise, consider those unmasked times in Queens or Gotham or in the Fortress of Solitude. Imagine them not doing, just being ordinary human beings, no one in particular.

We all fear being vulnerable, exposed as less than solid or coherent, shifting with changing conditions. At one point in the unfolding saga of Superman, he tells Lois Lane that Clark Kent is just two words, a simple fixed identity. In reality, he is "The Blur," the term used by a bystander who witnessed him in action. If we could see ourselves from out in space, we would all be blurs, just streams of experience.

Batman became a masked crusader after the murder of his parents. He vowed to avenge their death by dispensing justice. He trained for years, creating his identity as a positive form of revenge.

Peter Parker became Spider-Man after being bitten by a radioactive spider. We are all like this. We make do. We compensate. We build and refine our defense systems. And sometimes, if we learn to allow ourselves to be nobody, our wounds and seeming catastrophes become portals to a great new life.

Maybe superheroes express our yearning to soar above it all—to help this suffering world but also to transcend it. At first, many of us turn to a spiritual practice hoping for a way to smooth out our bumpy lives or at least find a little peace and ease. But for real peace and ease we must draw closer to life, especially our own lives. As we learn to allow ourselves to take time to do nothing, we come home to a presence that can hold all of our experience with kind acceptance. We learn to let go of our thinking and our stories. We learn to take off the cape and the mask, and just be no one.

For a time, allow yourself to sit and be still, not meditating but being soft, attending to what is happening without thinking. Notice the wise and loving presence that is always here.

4

Night in the Forest

Before his enlightenment, the man who would be the Buddha sat through a long dark night. According to ancient Buddhists texts, this night lasted for seven weeks, or forty-nine days. The reference to forty (or forty-nine) days is not to be taken literally but believed by scholars to mean a very long time, in the same way that Christian Bible stories speak of forty days in the desert and so on. Seven weeks in the dark. This conveys how it feels to be deeply and completely lost in the unknown, to be sitting in a place of vibrating, vulnerable uncertainty, your whole life and identity in question. And this is what the Buddha did. People tend to focus on the light, the glorious enlightenment, the radiant return to the world. It seems incidental that it appeared in the midst of the darkness. We relish the details of the story: Siddhartha Gautama, an Indian prince, left his palace (actually multiple palaces) and his family and a life of status and luxury to seek something that no one had ever found. It takes a long time to register, what feels more like forty years than forty days, that the real end of his quest was the darkness and solitude of the forest—not the knowing but the unknowing.

The Buddha sat down under the sheltering bodhi tree and opened up to life as if he were encountering it for the first time. We can begin to relate to this by remembering those times when we received a great hurt or shocking news and went off by ourselves. How strange and new life can seem, full of unknown powers. Abandoning all faith in the old forms and stories and established truths, he discovered a wild new kind of hope that was not a fixed belief but a willingness to be open to unforeseen possibility.

He was pulled into the forest by questions that came from the depths of his life. This questioning wasn't in words and thoughts, but in feelings that filled the body and charged the air around him. Why did he still suffer? Why did everybody suffer?

He questioned his whole life up to that point. What had he been doing with his life? He saw the swings between indulgence and austerity, from parties in harems to painful fasting. All of it came to nothing. And now stillness.

In the depths of an Indian forest, the man who wanted to wake up sat very still. He watched everything that happened inside and outside, sensing every sensation, feeling every feeling, listening to every sound. He observed his own thoughts the way Jane Goodall observed chimpanzees in the wild in Africa: with total patience and a willingness to suspend all conclusions, to just go on seeing.

"Quiet friend who has come so far, feel how your breathing makes more space around you," wrote the poet Rilke.[6]

Aware of his breath, aware of his solitude, the Buddha observed his own mind, seeing his many past lives. Even if you don't believe that people have more than one life, you know what it feels like to remember earlier times that may as well be past lives. The Buddha saw and felt the pain that comes from attachment to things and beings and relationships that change and are lost. Alone in the forest, he must have felt great grief, but he went on seeing. His sitting was a reckoning, a willingness to be completely open to suffering, seeking the root of it, sensing that the way out is down.

How can I claim to know any such thing about the Buddha's state? I simply take him at his word, that he made his journey to realization as an ordinary human, just like us. The story of his awakening isn't intended just for monastics or men or one culture or epoch. It is a map. Our living experience is the territory to be explored. Every step and every phase, including the dark time in the forest, is true in an outer sense—yes, he sat beneath a tree and among trees—and in an inner sense: he was willing to be lost in the woods.

Most of us know how it feels to lose things—people and relationships and stories that no longer seem true—to find ourselves alone in wild new territory. We know how it feels to lie awake in the dark. We listen to our breathing, our heartbeat, and the night sounds. But mostly we watch the mind spin, creating scenes, grasping for solutions and certainty, and finding none. We feel an ache in the heart and know that much of our furious activity has been an attempt to save us from the sensation of not knowing.

This feeling can be so piercing. We may think that we have missed the essential point of being alive. We were given one job—to be here and to pay attention—and we blew it. Looking back, we see that we were sidetracked time and again. We feel the knife twist of having wasted so much time *not* being here. To be where else exactly? We see now that we pursued one dream or need or idea after another, playing a part or pleasing a part of ourselves. Somehow we were distracted from doing what would be good for the whole. Weirdly, we realize that being fully present more often would have been so much less stressful and sad. There would have been so much less fighting and fleeing and freezing, so much more stillness and listening and opening to receive. How could there have been so few moments of this?

The practice that began with the Buddha sitting alone in the forest is a way of living our deepest questions. It is not a way of escaping, but a method of being true to ourselves, opening to our most profound insights and intentions without always rushing past them or explaining them away or casting them in a more flattering light or seeking to improve them by adding a motivational quote or two.

Just be still and see. Be willing to be what is, abandoning all hope of things being any other way. Don't try to let go. Just let things be. Dare to experience what presents itself. Let yourself sink into the sensation of being here just like this. Notice that this brings a different kind of hope that is not a fixed belief or image of what will come, but just a little flare or fizz. Realize that you can be open to an unthought-of possibility: something unexpected and good may come; there might be light in the midst of that darkness. And just for a moment, we may discover that pain is not the deepest thing in us. Love is. Real love, we discover, is not a romantic yearning but that fizz, that willingness to see how things turn out, that flash of luminous energy that lights us up from the inside.

As the Buddha sat meditating, he saw his past lives, watched karma playing out in lifetime after lifetime. Whether we believe in rebirth or not, we know how it feels to vividly remember scenes from the past. With a smell, a song, a change in the weather, we time-travel, remembering the exact taste of cold cider on a crisp October day or the warmth of a summer evening when we looked across a café table and realized that we were in love. We marvel every time this happens, that our felt experiences live on in us, waiting to be recalled.

But what exactly is being called? We are completely different people now. So much has changed, and yet this feeling, this essence of something remains. We know as we remember that it wasn't the form or the details, not the actual cider or sunset, but the spirit that was present. The Buddhists call this bodhi mind, our awakened or enlightened mind. And what is truly marvelous is that this is not something we need to acquire. It is our innate awareness, our capacity to open to receive life, to really be present and part of it.

For all our striving and yearning, in moments of deep remembering we know that what is most precious to us is something we glimpse or feel in short moments, often mundane in the telling—that one time in the kitchen with our mother or walking in the woods or sitting in a café listening and really hearing our daughter. What we remember as wondrous are not the words and the forms and the details, what you baked or what café, but the essence or spirit behind them. We remember moments when our heart or mind or heart-mind opened like a lens and took in something that felt real and true.

The Buddha sat still in the forest, open to every memory and every experience that arose within him. He was resolved to go on seeing and feeling until he discerned a deeper truth. Picture opening a faucet and watching until rusty water turns clear. His patient determination was not an act of will so much as an act of radical willingness to be with his experience without striving to fix or explain or defend, just watching with interest until clarity arose.

Eventually, the Buddha saw beneath the stream of thoughts and memories of past lives to discern the workings of karma. He saw that every action, including the subtle action of thought, has a consequence, creating ripples that fan out in unexpected ways, impacting our lives and the lives of others. He saw how thoughts become habitual, shaping our beliefs and characters and ultimately our destinies. He saw how seemingly tiny inner actions, a clinging or the opposite, a letting go of an attachment to a view, can contract or open us. He saw how the act of seeing itself can change everything.

Pay attention, be willing to see and feel what comes up without judgment, and eventually you will see more and see deeper. You will notice a witnessing awareness inside that is light and kind. For a second or two, you will experience that you are more than your sorrow and fear and trauma, more than anything that happened to you. This awareness feels unlimited, and although you don't know how this can be, you feel that this awareness may be an opening, a glimpse of sunlight behind the clouds, a way to be free.

It is important to remember that the Buddha's quest didn't end with an answer or a promise, but in a question. It ended in his willingness to *be in question*, to be the subject of the search. He had to be willing to let go of all the old forms and established truths, to be the unknown land, the dark forest. He let go of everything he thought he knew and everything he thought he was. Sitting very still under the sheltering tree, he watched his thoughts, noting the myriad ways over myriad lifetimes that he dealt with fear and anxiety and loss, sometimes fighting and striving, sometimes running away, sometimes denying. Quiet but courageous, he sought the deeper truth of his life.

The root of the word *courage* is *cor*—the Latin for "heart." The original meaning was not heroism in the sense of brandishing a sword, but heartfulness or living from the whole of ourselves, in touch with the truth of our deepest felt experience. This can take a long time. It helps to know this, and that it is a practice of moments. It also helps to know that there is a deeper presence in us that sees without judgment.

As the sky grew lighter, the Buddha grew lighter. His enlightenment was not a thought, not a set of beliefs, but an action, a dawning and opening to a truth that is beyond thought. During his long night, the Buddha watched his thoughts, saw where they came from and where they went. He watched lifetime after lifetime unspool, how each life was braided with grief and haunted by loneliness and fear. The root meaning of *grief* is "weight or gravity," and the Buddha must have felt a heavy pull in his bones. So many lives. So much suffering.

Enlightenment is a lightening up. A veil is lifted. The heavy sadness of always misunderstanding is dispelled. The Buddha saw that under each lifetime, each painful story, there was exactly the same suffering. The circumstances were different, and the styles of grasping and avoidance varied, but all of it was driven by the delusion that we are separate entities, fending off danger and striving to pull in the love and other nutrients we need.

We are heavily defended creatures. We can't help this. We are wired this way. Even our cells defend themselves against invaders. The Buddha was said to have cosmic vision so he could see defensiveness at work on every scale and level. He could see that the ego and all of its ways are a defense against psychic pain. Humans long to open and connect with others, to be seen and loved, and yet there is this elaborate system that defends against it. What can help? Attention.

We can picture the Buddha as an archaeologist, patiently and attentively working his way down and down into the heart of life, attending to each artifact that is unearthed with care and curiosity. He was on a quest for freedom, and he worked with the blend of patience and concentration that a person might put into tunneling out of prison with a spoon. All his bridges were burned. There was nowhere for him to go but here, and nothing for him to do but to seek the deeper story under the surface—the truth buried under the misconceptions and false narratives.

The Buddha left the palace and the known world of his status and his teachers for the wilderness. He allowed himself to be completely vulnerable, completely undefended against reality. He didn't deny the darkness. He sat down with it, and he found a light in the midst of it. This great letting go is part of awakening to our fight against reality. When we turn our attention to ourselves, we discover that much of our suffering comes from our attempts to defend ourselves against pain and suffering.

Giving up our defenses can bring a slow-spreading relief, like the gentle calm that follows tears. When we allow ourselves to be vulnerable, just seeing and feeling what is there to be seen and felt and just there for all the world to see with no excuses and no commentary, we open to a new relationship with reality. We are reconciled, not defeated but brave: here I am. In the end, the Buddha split off from his friends and sat down beneath a tree, vowing not to rise again until he had found another way to be alive, fully and authentically here, not repeating the old patterns. He was over suffering—no doubts, no last arguments playing out in his head, no going back. He didn't seek a new way to handle suffering. He had tried everything, and now he was ready to be gone.

He didn't know what would come next. He just knew he was ready—ready to pull his attention and his energy away from the old narratives, ready to open to life. So he sat there opening, watching without fixed expectation. In the middle of the night, the devil Mara loomed up like an angry orange fire, conjuring seductive and terrifying visions, seeking to trigger reactions. The Buddha calmly reached down and touched the earth, affirming his right to be sitting there, to fully belong to life without fear.

"You don't know the size of my army," he told Mara. Life was with him. Truth was with him.

We are not alone. Ancient stories tell us that the tree the Buddha chose to sit beneath on his great quest for enlightenment burst into bloom when the Buddha arrived. Myriad other trees and plants and creatures took notice and rejoiced in riotous, colorful ways. The descriptions seem fantastical until we remember how it feels to leave the dark little kingdom of the head and open to presence. Letting go of our thoughts, we look around and notice the sky and the trees. We smell crisp fall air and hear voices in the distance. Life is always fresh and unknown, we remember, always offering itself to us. Making this movement of return to sensation, to presence, we too are welcomed into the party of creation.

And on the night of his enlightenment, lonely isolation and striving ceased. He took root in a greater life and bloomed. Going forth on his great quest for truth, his name was Siddhartha Gotama. This was his birth name, along with Shakyamuni, because he was part of the Shakya clan. But upon waking, none of those descriptions defined him anymore. Centuries after his death, he was called the Buddha, the Awakened One. He called himself the Tathagata, which means one "thus gone and thus arrived"—one who has gone beyond all that bound and defined him in the past, arriving someplace unbounded and free.

This "thus gone and thus arrived" formulation describes the experience of enlightenment. And yet we can relate to it here and now in our ordinary lives. Most of us have had moments when we suddenly see a truth about ourselves, a way that we cling or contract in our relationships and in life. In those moments when we really see and fully accept what we see, we move out of an old way of being and arrive somewhere new. We feel more aware and more alive, not as limited by our histories and beliefs. We know that certain things happened, but we don't feel defined by that. It is as if we have slipped out of a net and arrived somewhere new, feet on the ground, senses alive, present and aware that we are aware in a living world.

So what happened after the Buddha achieved enlightenment? Ancient stories tell us that the first thing he did is stand and gaze at the tree that had sheltered and supported him during his long night. For seven days before he left the forest, the Awakened One faced the tree, giving her the finest, and really the only, gift he had to give: the gift of his full attention. As extreme as this gift of seeing seems, we all know how it feels to wake up, if only for a moment. It feels like arriving in a new world. A world that has always been here, waiting for us to notice. The old stories describe that tree bursting into bloom, and the whole world of creation flowering and making a wild rumpus, celebrating his awakening. This sounds like a tale for children, but this is how it can feel to be completely open and attentive, not thinking of some way life could be better or worse and so ever-so-slightly out of sync.

Awakening means awakening to the truth that we are part of nature. We are nature. Our changing mind states, including all our feelings—even the most difficult—and all the thoughts and stories that attach to them, are natural, just as the weather is natural. Grief and anxiety and depression and anger are as natural as rain. Our thinking and all the defensive machinations of the ego are natural, too.

And another truth is that there isn't just one awakening—and not just one kind. The wisdom of enlightenment is often likened to a jewel with many facets. It is not just a single blinding light from above, but many moments of seeing and realization many times. It blooms inside us as those moments accumulate, illuminating and so transforming our suffering. We tend to think of spiritual progress as ascending a mountain, but we may actually awaken downward into the depths of our lives, descending from our thoughts and stories into the authentic experience of being alive. Moments of true seeing reveal that what is most essential in us is not a fixed thing, some ultimate true identity, but our fluid nature and our capacity to be constantly aware of a life that is always changing.

Awareness grows as we practice noticing it. We begin to discover that there is a kind of resolution in us that is not a matter of words and vows but a hunger to open the lens of our being, to be more aware more often. It is as if we become magnetized to moments of presence, realizing drop by drop, moment by moment that there is a greater life for us to live. It is astonishing to realize that life is not out there in some other better place, but here. And the effort needed is not striving, but giving up striving, being willing to just sit here and be.

We already know this. It's a matter of knowing what we know. When we are truly present for others, conveying that we are all here for them with all the time in the world, they feel it. They relax and open and reveal their truths. And this is so when we grant this kind of patient interest to ourselves.

Ultimately, awakening is a destructive act. It blows away what we believe to be true and possible. The good news is that it is a little like waking up from a bad dream and finding yourself safe and alive, blinking in the morning light. You might think that this is just a tad simplistic. Aren't some of the monsters that chase us all too real? Aren't there terrible partners and children and jobs and too much stress and too little money? And isn't there also injustice and a pandemic and all kinds of other mental and physical health problems? Yes, of course, and so much more!

But in my worst nightmares, the worst thing is the haunting isolation. Not only am I lost in a strange place but I am completely alone—the lines are down, the phone is lost, and often I have no voice to scream for help or make a call. In moments of awakening, I still in actual fact have voice issues, but I remember that I live in a shared world. I feel the air moving in and out of my lungs, sense the air on my skin, and remember without any words that I am alive. In sickness and in health, I am in a long-term committed relationship with life.

During the long night that preceded the Buddha's awakening, he touched the earth. He remembered that there was more to him than his own worst fears. No matter what his mind conjured up, he was also supported, given air and shelter and witness, beloved on the earth. In my quietest moments, I also feel the life all around me, supporting and nourishing me. I remember that every time my plans and dreams have come tumbling down, I awaken to the living truth that there is an awareness or presence in me that is still here, watching. I remember that I am more than my dreams and worst fears, that I am in fact dwelling in the midst of a great and mysterious and in every sense moving world. In spite of everything, something in me wants to open and be part of it. A new life is possible.

One useful way to think of the ego is as a defense system aimed at protecting us against pain, particularly the pain of being no one. We are constantly renewing our sense of self, and that self continues to validate itself by *doing* things, aiming to be better and better at life. The ego claims everything, including spiritual practices, including mindfulness meditation, as a means of self-perfection.

And we may improve a little. We may feel a little more peaceful, a little less stressed or quick to anger. Being a little bit happier a little more often is a very good thing. No wonder spiritual books are marketed promising such results—often in a certain number of days or weeks.

Yet, even as we buy the book or sign up for the course, we sense that we are still seeking to establish a firm place to stand on shifting ground. Nothing we do can really stop life and time, and we know it. When we are still, even for a short time, we notice that the ego is constantly striving to get to a better place where it can rest. It is not at peace in *this* place, and it imagines it will be happy in *another* place. It yearns for a better identity, the identity of one who has arrived. Yet deep down, we still sense our sorrow and fear of being no one.

Remember that in ancient times, when people first heard of the Buddha's teachings on the emptiness or changeable, striving nature of the ego self, it was considered most auspicious to feel not joy but terror—perhaps intuiting what must come. The ego must volunteer to abdicate the throne in the center of your life. It must agree to die and let you be no one at least some of the time.

The ego always seeks a way to wiggle out of this death. It wants a little more peace and ease, better focus. But as we practice being present we come to the realization that real peace and freedom come in those moments when we are no one. We notice that when we are more awake we are not thinking of a self. We have the most amazing insight. The death of the ego, those moments of being nobody, are not deadness. It means awakening to the flow of life.

Reflect and tell about moments of no self or ego death on any given day. Look for these glimpses in simple, forgettable tasks—cooking, cleaning, walking. Notice moments of ease and opening, moments when we forget ourselves and let life flow in.

5

Elizabeth

The summer after I graduated from college, days before I moved to New York City to launch a real adult life, I saw a ghost—an apparition, a spirit, an angel. Decades later, I am still not sure what to call it or where it came from. But I can still see her as if she appeared at the foot of my bed last night. And I'll never forgot what she told me.

It happened in the big old house my family moved to when I was fourteen years old, after my mother decided that our first house, a cozy brick ranch house designed by an uncle and largely built by my father, was no longer big enough. I was told the big house was a bargain because the previous owners were highly motivated to sell.

There was something gloomy and oppressive about the place. The kitchen was modernized, but the rest of the house was full of dark wainscoting. The diagonal placement of the fireplace and the angles of the rooms were off-kilter so that doors didn't shut tight. I left my bedroom door ajar because, if I didn't, the old latch unlatched and the door creaked open in the middle of the night. Even my father, the most pragmatic and cheerful of men, admitted that the dark and narrow upstairs hallway felt "ominous."

The front room upstairs, the former main bedroom, became my room. It had three huge windows that overlooked the street, so it should have been cheerful but instead was the gloomiest room of all. It was dominated by a wooden bed with an elaborately carved headboard that touched the ceiling and a high footboard. It had big carved urns on top of the bedpost finials and looked like something a literary character would sleep in—a young Dracula or Jane Eyre, as she listened to the strange sounds in Mr. Rochester's mansion.

The family joked that this bedroom was mine because I was the only one who fit the bed. Brackets had been added in the frame to fit a modern mattress, but it was too short for anyone over 5'6" or so, and that was everyone except me. But I also fit the bed because I was the most mystical, ethereal, dramatic. Like many adolescents, I harbored the sense that I was secretly capable of a greater life, and I cloaked this sense under a protective layer of darkness. If I were a teenager today, I would probably have adopted the goth style. In those days, I was drawn to dark, brooding hippie poets like Jim Morrison.

Hoping to make my room a psychedelic sanctum completely separate from the rest of the house, I persuaded my father to bolt a three-foot black light to the ceiling. This plunged most of the room into darkness and cast certain things—anything white and the fluorescent paint in my psychedelic posters—in an eerie ultraviolet glow. I remember lying in that bed reading books like *The Doors of Perception* by Aldous Huxley and *Siddhartha* by Hermann Hesse. I remember staring at a poster of Jim Morrison making a beckoning gesture, wondering how I would ever find my way into the magic inside life. In those days, there were no owls flying in to invite a kid to Hogwarts School of Witchcraft and Wizardry. I was sure it would take drastic measures—leaving home to be a wandering ascetic like Siddhartha perhaps, travel to remote nooks and crannies of the world, shaman guides, strange rituals and potions—to lift me out of the confining shell of my little self.

The summer after I graduated from college, the black light and Jim Morrison poster were gone. But so was my inner confidence. Under all that high-school imagining there had been an intuition that glowed like white sheets under black light. I sensed that the truth could not be thought. It could not be conveyed by any verbal proposition or formula because it did not consist of fact. You perceived, received, felt the inner meaning of life. I wasn't sure how, but I sensed that I was made for this.

After college, I brimmed with ideas, but I no longer trusted or even knew how I felt. I planned to move to New York City, like someone numb with cold heading toward a distant fire. I didn't know what I would find, but I had to head toward life. I planned to stay with a college friend while I looked for a job in publishing. Neither the friend nor the plan was right for me. I realize now that my heart was full of foreboding. There was truth waiting that I didn't want to let in.

The ancient Celts spoke of "thin places"—places where the boundaries between worlds, between day and night, sleep and waking, what is seen and unseen, are more porous. I decided our house might be a thin place. And looking back, I think I might have been a thin place too. Certainly it was a time when I was vulnerable to the unknown.

I awoke in the night with a start to see a young woman standing at the foot of my bed. She had long wavy hair and very fine features. She was very beautiful but seemed to be made of white mist, like a very fine sculpture in dry ice. She was wearing a long Victorian dress. To this day I can see the eyelets in the lace. She smiled at me and told me her name was Elizabeth. I remember gasping for breath. My heart raced and my lungs burned as if I were running hard, yet my legs felt paralyzed.

Years later, I learned that paralysis is common during ghostly encounters, as is this detail: I didn't see her feet. It wasn't just a matter of the high footboard. When people see ghosts, according to the paranormal researchers I interviewed, they don't report seeing their feet. Most unusual was the way she looked directly at me and addressed me. Most ghosts are unseeing, literally haunted. And then there was her message.

Still smiling at me, she said, "I came to tell you that if you don't want your body, there are others who do."

A jolt of terror lit me up inside like fireworks. "No!" welled up from the depths of my being. My mind filled entirely with one aim, one thought that pushed out all other thoughts and unthinkable possibilities: "I want this body! I want this life." There was a surge of energy, a fierce certainty that I would fight to the death for this life. My deepest instincts were rallying to my defense.

On the night the Buddha achieved enlightenment, he reached down and touched the earth, asking it to bear witness to his right to be there, sitting under that tree. It is traditionally taught that the Buddha was asking the earth to acknowledge his many lifetimes of seeking. But I believe he was also reaching down to claim his deeper nature, calling the whole of himself to the great task of awakening.

It would be years before I encountered the symbolic act of the Buddha touching the earth as he faced the demon Mara. But it perfectly captured the sense I had of touching the earth of my life that night.

This pale messenger presented me with a reality beyond my wildest imagination. Her message exploded my sense of the possibilities and preciousness of my life. Suddenly, I was a resident of the world of the living, and something in my deeper nature—something that connected me to the whole of nature—rose to my defense.

For a time when I was a little girl, I had a black panther named Striker as an invisible friend. We would run and climb trees. Faced with imaginary enemies, we would crouch and pounce with catlike grace. Striker was my own metaphor for joy, passion, and embodiment. That night, without a single word intruding, I remembered what it means to be embodied. Our human truth is not separate from it. Understanding draws on the experience of standing under, receiving the truth that rains down on you and into you. In a flash of terror, I realized we may dwell in the midst of other worlds. But the meaning I was searching for was in me.

Still smiling, and speaking in a soothing voice, Elizabeth explained that she didn't live in the house but nearby. She told me I could reach her if I needed her—and I had the impression that she meant she lived in the house next door. This proved wrong, which I will explain in a bit. Even now I can see how serene and light she looked as she backed away in that dark old house.

I don't know how long it took me to peel my frozen limbs off the bed and run down the hall to wake my mother. My father was often away in those days. Gasping, heart pounding, I choked out what happened: "You might think I'm crazy, but I've just seen a ghost."

"I don't think you're crazy," she said. Inviting me to come sit next to her in the bed, she told me that one night when she had been alone in the big old house she had woken up in the middle of the night to see a column of white fog hovering in the doorway. "It was so strange," she said. "I'm the type who has to investigate, so I walked toward it. I felt so cold and sad as I drew close, then it disappeared."

In the days that followed, I heard other stories. A houseguest had reported hearing footsteps in the upstairs hall and a heavy scraping sound like a trunk being dragged across the attic floor. My parents came home from a monthlong vacation and felt a presence in the house. "It was the strangest thing," said my father. "It was as if someone wearing violet cologne had just left the room. Your mother and I looked at each other without saying a word, each of us sensing that someone was there." I was the only one who saw an apparition.

After that night, I couldn't move to New York fast enough. I made a wordless vow never to speak of the experience or even think of it. But it trailed after me, a riddle I hadn't completely understood. I worked in publishing, then in the movie business, and finally became a writer—always striving in the same spirit of drawing closer to the fire, seeking a more vivid experience of life.

Not long after I moved, my parents sold the house—for a song, they said. Sadness and mishaps befell the new owners, who sold the house to others, who also came to grief and sold the house. My mother speculated that there was something sinister about the place. It was often for sale. Recently I visited my hometown and saw the sign was up again.

At what I thought was a safe distance and in good company, I sometimes allowed myself to feel what happened. Friends sometimes asked me if I thought the apparition might be a guardian spirit or angel. Wherever she came from, whether some other dimension or the depths of my own psyche, maybe she came to help.

A decade after I saw Elizabeth, I left corporate life to be a freelance writer. I moved from the Upper West Side to the gritty East Village, so the fire I drew close to turned out to be the trash can fires the winos lit around Tompkins Square Park. But I felt bohemian and brave. *New York Magazine* gave me an assignment to cover a séance that was held regularly on the Upper West Side. I sat in a comfortable living room, watching as intelligent-seeming people sought guidance from a man who went into a trance to purportedly channel wisdom from an ancient being. I was convinced the man was a fraud, and I tried to ask probing questions to try to prove it.

"I have a question for you," said the man, when he came out of his trance. "Who is Elizabeth? In the atmosphere all around you, I hear the name Elizabeth." All my bright questions blew out.

A few years later, I received an assignment from a now defunct science and science-fiction magazine called *Omni* to write about how researchers use the methods of science to track down ghosts. I leapt at the chance. In addition to interviewing paranormal researchers and skeptics and doing research of my own, I visited the scene of a few hauntings and paranormal investigations. One was a rambling apartment on Washington Square. As I sat at a kitchen table drinking coffee, "Kathleen" (she didn't want her real name used in the article) described what had happened to her one night in October 1973. She told me she heard the front door slam. Thinking it was her sister and preoccupied with the dinner party they had planned, she rushed happily toward the door. In the dusty rose-colored hallway she froze, and all the happy images in her mind went dark.

"There was a hunched-over figure in a black robe," said Kathleen (I quote from my 1988 *Omni* article). "I thought it was a robber, though it seemed very sick or old." She turned on the light and watched the figure creep toward the bathroom down the hall. She called to her mother who was in her bedroom up the hall, asking her who had just entered the apartment. "Nobody," her mother answered. "It was almost as if the figure was absorbing light instead of reflecting it," the woman told me. "But even then, I never thought of a ghost."

The following night Kathleen looked up from the sofa to see her mother standing in the doorway shaking. She told Kathleen she had heard a whooshing sound in the hall and looked up to see a "transparent blackness" passing down the hallway toward the bathroom. She yelled "Kathleen! Kathleen!" and ran after the shadow, only to find nothing there. Soon enough Michaeleen Maher, a family friend with a PhD in parapsychology, heard about these incidents. Equipped with a Geiger counter, infrared photography equipment, and a team of volunteers, Maher attempted to use the tools and techniques of science to investigate. The results were suggestive but maddeningly elusive in scientific terms. There was a "parabola of fog" in an infrared photo of the hallway, and a flurry of Geiger clicks in a particular spot, but nothing that could not be ruled out by ordinary explanations.

I remember sitting with Kathleen and Maher in the kitchen of that apartment on Washington Square. In the years after the haunting, Kathleen became an accomplished photographer and her smoky, evocative photos lined the walls. She, Maher, and I studied the infrared photo with the parabolic arc of fog. They pointed out a dark circle.

"To me it looks like a black face up close to the camera," said Kathleen. Maher said that one of the psychics she brought in reported seeing the figure of an African American. Kathleen and Maher acted out how the mysterious figure moved up the hall. The tour ended in her late mother's room at a window overlooking Washington Square Park. What Kathleen explained next shifted my perspective for good.

Directly across the street from the window stood a massive old elm tree. Kathleen said that according to her research, the last person to be hanged in New York City was hanged from that tree. She was an African American woman who had worked as a servant in one of the grand buildings lining the park. The conversation rushed on: Kathleen saying that ghosts open up a world of forces and influences science can't understand; Maher suggesting that someday science may have tools fine enough to collect physical evidence for such phenomena.

I kept thinking of that servant, hanged for stealing. I wondered if there might be situations so grave and critical they are impressed on us—and on the world we live in—by extraordinary means.

I learned there are many cases of haunting seen by hundreds of people—the Allied landing at Normandy on D-Day is one. I wondered if we were asking the wrong questions, looking at the experience in the wrong way. Maybe the focus should be shifted from a ghostly messenger and where she came from and turned back to the one who perceived the experience. I found it amazing that we humans are capable of such perceptions. We are larger than we know.

I was certain of the reality of my experience. Yet I also came away siding with the skeptics. As Ray Hyman, professor of psychology at the University of Oregon, explained to me, even the most rigorous of these investigations "are historical investigations, not true scientific investigations at all." It all comes down to testimony, stories. No researcher has ever been able to capture a ghost by way of an experiment that can be repeated in a lab.

Science could tell me nothing about my experience. Very slowly, it dawned on me that its meaning might arise in the space between extremes of affirmation and denial. It might come to me in the midst of my life as I lived it, slowly opening over time like the meaning in a story or a myth.

My article on modern-day ghost hunters became a front-page story, and I was invited to participate in an experiment in a famous haunted location—something that was later reenacted in a television show called *Unsolved Mysteries*. In an attempt at scientific purity, I was told nothing about where I was going or what exactly I was going to be doing, only that a group of us would be leaving after dark and spending the night.

I remember standing outside my apartment in the East Village in downtown Manhattan, alive with uncertainty and anticipation. As I watched the punk kids, artists, and all the other members of the wild and raggedy East Village scene pass, I registered that I didn't know what I was meant to do here on earth, that probably few people did. But I sensed it had something to do with bearing witness to the life I was given to live, with really digging into it and learning what there was to learn. Although it would take years to let this truth soak in, I realized that night that we are meant to follow the flow of our lives, to be with our embodied experience in all its imperfection—but also to turn our attention to the one who knows.

In the van with parapsychologist Maher and others, I learned that I was to be a control in an experiment that involved leading a group of psychics through the General Wayne Inn in Merion, Pennsylvania. My job was to sit for hours on the cellar steps. One by one, the psychics were led from the attic to the basement. Backs turned to me, facing the shadowy wine cellar, several psychics gasped or murmured that they sensed something. Yet in spite of this uncanny confirmation, the investigation was scientifically inconclusive.

As the sky grew light, everyone in the search party gathered in the bar. The manager and bartender offered us coffee and drinks. They had liked my *Omni* article and agreed with its skeptical conclusion. I marveled that I had sat much of the night in the basement, unable to sense the presence of any of the unknown forces around me. What I didn't tell them was that it had felt strangely peaceful and intimate. I remember sitting there breathing, registering that I was alive, in my body and breathing, and yet I wasn't as fully alive, not as sensitive and aware, as I could be. A new kind of questioning dawned that would take years to break the surface of consciousness. I came to understand that there was another kind of investigation to be done—not outside but inside.

If you don't want your body, there are others who do. I once heard that the Indians of North America thought that the invading European settlers were possessed by the wendigo, a malevolent, flesh-eating spirit that took over their bodies and drove them to consume the lives of others, to consume the earth. I began to see how easily we can lose our sense of being embodied in this world in normal circumstances—taken over by the spirits of anger, fear, righteousness. I realized that it is very easy to lose your life before you die.

Over the years, the warning Elizabeth uttered rained down, soaked in, led me to understand a truth that is situational, personal, perceived in the moment. The angel, the ghost, the spirit that is Elizabeth showed me that the experience of embodiment leads us back to the marvel of perceiving and the mystery of the one who knows. She showed me that the richer, deeper life I longed for when I was young is available here and now in the vulnerability and imperfection of this body in the present moment . . . if I want it.

"An unsolved mystery is a thorn in the heart."

The author Joyce Carol Oates used this sentence as a prompt for students in her creative writing class at Princeton University. I used this exercise in my mindful writing workshops again and again. Often, at New York Insight Meditation Society or the Rubin Museum of Art, I would invite people to start by coming to their senses, writing down just what they could see, hear, smell, taste, and sense of the world around us on the page, letting their direct observations speak for themselves. I invite you to try this now. Setting aside ten minutes (and understanding that this can be five minutes or fifteen or twenty in practice), just list without editing what is present inside and out: snow gently falling, the warmth of the coffee mug in your hands, the heaviness of fatigue.

Take a break. Stand up and stretch or have a cup of tea or go for a walk. Allow yourself to be present without trying hard to pay attention. Later, give yourself twenty minutes or so (it can be less or more) to try this as a prompt for reflection: allow yourself to be present to an unsolved mystery in your own life. Just note the mystery—or mysteries—in the same simple and direct way you note sense perceptions. Start small, if you think you have no mysteries in your life: Why did two socks go into the dryer and only one came out—where did that sock go? More and deeper mysteries will follow.

Using this prompt in groups large and small, and listening to people who share afterward, I have learned that we all hold unsolved mysteries. A person may start out with a seemingly mundane if upsetting question: *I wonder who dented my car and drove away?* Yet inevitably, if we keep questioning with an open attention, we begin wondering about the mystery of being alive. *Why do people do such things?* Such a reflection can deepen into wonderment at how interconnected we are or how one thing leads to another.

Ultimately, we ourselves are the mystery. Our lives are so much deeper and broader and wilder than we think they are most of the time. Was that a ghost? Had it been a strange and particularly vivid kind of dream? Was it a ghost or something far more benevolent and light-filled, perhaps a guardian or a guide?

Giving yourself some time to wonder, even about long-ago losses, can make life surprisingly wonderful. We see that the seeming "facts" of our lives can give way like the rungs of an old ladder under the weight of an open question. Why did that relationship end? Notice that gentle wondering, mindful investigation, terrifying or confining, like being grilled at a police station. Gently, like a river flowing toward the sea, it opens to the biggest and juiciest question of all: *Who am I?* Notice how this great question enlivens and awakens you to the mystery of life that is pouring in through every sense door.

As the Zen saying goes: Great questioning, great awakening; little questioning, little awakening; no questioning, no awakening.

PART TWO

Heart

Exploring our sensations can lead on to the deeper world of our feelings—not our ordinary emotions and thoughts, not our usual likes and dislikes, but essential feelings for the basic goodness and value of being alive. Sensation is the pressure of hands kneading dough, the warmth of the oven, the smell of fresh-baked bread. Feeling is the memory of baking with your mother on a winter day, and the sense of the goodness and preciousness of this seemingly ordinary act.

6

French Lessons

One October morning, I experienced a moment of grace. It happened as I was walking my black Labrador retriever Shadow on one of those warm autumn days when everything looks edged in gold. But I was shuffling along like a waif in a storm because I had just learned that a project I had counted on had fallen through.

Shadow staged a sit-down strike when we came to a little lake. Head high, back straight, she refused to budge until she had a chance to explore the shore. So I stood and waited. A pair of white swans and a dozen Canada geese were gliding over quiet water that mirrored trees ablaze with yellow and scarlet leaves. It struck me that there was a living presence, a shining awareness behind this world.

My heart reached out. It was like a fist unclenching. It let go of all the ideas I had been carrying about what success and fulfillment are supposed to look like, scattering them on the water like bread crumbs for the geese.

"Thy will, not mine, be done," I said, and I meant it. There was a lightening inside. It was as if I had walked out of a small, dark room into the beautiful flow of life around me.

Later that day a friend phoned and urged me to call Chuck Hornsby at Lyon Travel in Brattleboro, Vermont. Hornsby was organizing a group of wine journalists to fly to the South of France for a week to attend a program at the Université du Vin. The journalists were to visit famous vineyards and winemakers in Provence and taste the spicy, complex Côtes du Rhône that many experts believe to be among the greatest wines in the world.

"But I've never written about wine," I told my friend. "I write about books and the search for truth."

"Well, *in vino veritas*," my friend replied.

Still under the spell of what had happened by the lake, I called Chuck Hornsby. To my amazement, he asked me if I could be ready to go in ten days. At dinner I told my husband and daughter that I had to fly to Provence.

"And I'm sure you will someday," murmured my husband.

I tried to explain.

"I don't think God is sending you Air France tickets to teach you a lesson about the goodness of life," countered my husband.

"Strangely enough, that's exactly what I think is happening," I answered.

My ten-year-old daughter reminded me to bring her back a present.

I met Chuck, a lean, crisp New Englander with a white mustache, at the train station in the walled medieval city of Avignon, the papal seat and center of Christendom in the fourteenth century. He loaded me and several of the wine journalists into a van and drove north to Rochegude, a tiny village lined with ancient buildings of yellow Provençal stone. Chuck informed me that Thomas Jefferson favored the wines of this region. Jefferson's worldliness amazed me; I couldn't imagine how any wine from this remote place would have reached him.

We crested a hilltop and drove through vast wooden gates into the cobblestone courtyard of the Château de Rochegude, now a four-star

Relais & Châteaux hotel. Night had fallen. I hopped out of the van and looked up at the ruins of the twelfth-century tower, remembering that there is nothing like a long trip to an exotic place to make us long for what is cozy and familiar. All I wanted was a hot bath and warm bed.

But I forced myself to meet the group for dinner. On the way to the dining room I passed through the Salon Cheminée, a chamber dominated by a vast fireplace and hung with ancient scrolls emblazoned with papal seals. Here, where waiters now stand at attention, was once the ecclesiastical court for the popes of Avignon. I wondered how the popes would have judged me.

As waiters glided around the table pouring wine, we introduced ourselves and described what we hoped to see and write about. Trying for a tone of sophisticated nonchalance, I announced to this group of professional oenophiles that I knew next to nothing about wine but that I was hoping for a spiritual epiphany.

"I guess your assignment is harder than ours," ventured someone after a long pause.

During our conversation, we were served a "light meal" that started with foie gras and proceeded through an array of delicious and mysterious dishes that culminated in the mildly humiliating trial of the cheese course. A stern-faced young woman wheeled a cart filled with dozens of cheese right up to me in spite of all my mental efforts to will her to move on to someone else.

"Madame?"

After the briefest bout of paralysis. I pointed at a chèvre. She stared at me with what seemed to be a mix of incredulity and barely concealed disgust at my lame choice. Finally, she cut me a slice and waited for me to choose again, and again. I tried to point with stony assurance.

The next morning, as I layered on sweaters and scarves against the cold, I armed myself with one of my favorite quotes: "Adventure is just discomfort in retrospect." This was the one thing I knew for sure. The sky was gray and the wind was howling when we arrived at the massive Château de Suze-la-Rousse, home of the Université du Vin. After a brief tour, we were ushered into a tasting amphitheater, which had tiers of desks outfitted with little sinks. Here we examined various Rhône wines for brilliance, richness, and intensity of color.

I held my glass by the stem and squinted at it, copying the people around me. I practiced swirling the glass to release the bouquet, or nose, of the wine.

"What are you getting?" asked our teacher.

"Lots of black fruit," said one voice.

"Black pepper," said another.

I learned that wines carry the scent of many things, from leather and game to mushroom, herbs, and the oak of the casks. The other journalists sloshed the wine over their palates to assess its weight, richness, depth, and balance. They spoke gravely of finish, or how long the taste of a sip lingered in the mouth. I was struck dumb by how much I couldn't taste.

During break, Jonathon Alsop, a wine journalist from Boston, assured me that although there is a science to making and tasting wine, it is an inescapably personal art as well. "Wine is of the earth," he said. "It has the vital force so it can stir our memory of things in life that we love." Over the course of the afternoon, I began to understand that the fermentation process is really a subtle alchemy that inflects simple grape juice with flavors that can move us the way the tang in the air on an autumn night might remind us of our first love. Tasting wine is a way to taste life.

At the end of the day, we descended into a vast wine cellar. We stood in near darkness on an earthen floor, surrounded by racks of rare wine, many of them hundreds of years old. "Remember that some of these wines are still alive and evolving," whispered one journalist, as if he might wake them. "And some are already dead."

"But how can you tell which wines will live and which will die?" I asked.

"Nobody knows," said someone else. A seemingly powerful, well-structured wine can fade while another opens up with each passing year, softening, deepening, and growing more interesting. It is a mystery. Just as it is with people.

Several days later, in the vineyards of Château La Nerthe in the famous wine village of Châteauneuf-du-Pape, I learned what I had come to France to learn. In the modern winery, I watched workers zipping around on forklift trucks, stepped over enormous hoses spewing wine, stared up at gleaming stainless steel silos. I passed through cold, cavernous halls of oak barrels where the wine is "racked" for aging and listened to people endlessly discuss technical details of winemaking in French and English. Someone invited me to stick my head into the porthole of a 50-hectoliter storage tank to smell "the sheer grapiness of it." I did. "Look at Tracy," said Alsop with a smile. "She's passed straight from hopes of an epiphany to disgust."

I laughed but at the same time was overwhelmed with the sense that I had traveled here under false pretenses. I had been floating along, vaguely hoping that at some point ordinary experience would be pierced by a greater awareness, like that moment of grace I had experienced at the lake. I had been so sure that I was being led. Now I felt like a child tagging along with the adults.

I wandered out to the terrace of the château and took in a landscape that might have inspired Vincent van Gogh. Not yet touched by frost, the vineyards were gold and seemed lit from underneath. The late afternoon sky was azure, and the clouds were lavender and molten pink. In the distance were stands of tall cypress trees and columns of workers harvesting olives. Lavender, thyme, rosemary, sage, and oregano, the *herbes de Provence*, scented the air. I had a thought as soft and fleeting as the perfume in the breeze: I had been dreaming and now I was awake. The process of awakening—like winemaking—is an alchemy that changes you, bringing the flavor of life inside.

Jay Fedigan, a friendly photographer from Boston, waved for me to come down into the vineyard. I was amazed that the gnarly vines were not rooted in the soil at all, but stood like rough fence posts in a field of big quartz stones in sandy red clay. At the Université du Vin, people had spoken reverently of old vines that grew in poor soil on steep slopes with no irrigation. I learned that conditions are deliberately made difficult in vineyards like this one. The yields of such vines are very low compared to the lush growth of more fertile fields, yet the grapes that survive have a very full, clear, concentrated flavor. It is the wines from these grapes that have the potential for greatness.

Fedigan urged me to pick up some stones and smell. He explained that the grapes carry the surrounding *terrior*—the soil and everything that touches them as they grow. I breathed in the spice, peppery warmth of the south. I felt the thrill of returning to my senses, of emerging from the small world of my hopes and fears into the larger world of air, rustling vines, and rocky soil beneath my feet. I was glad to be on an earth that knows how suffering can be transformed into strength and beauty, how hard times can be the ground for the deepest and purest joy.

"Today we have gathered and see that the cycles of life continue." Adapted from the Mohawk, this Thanksgiving greeting to the world offers thanks to the People, to Mother Earth and all her plants and herbs and creatures, to the Sun, the Moon, the Stars, the Waters, the Four Winds, and the Teachers. The Keepers of the Eastern Door, the most easterly section of the Haudenosaunee or Iroquois Confederacy, these were the Indigenous Americans of northern New York State, around Lake Ontario and the St. Lawrence River, the region where I grew up. Other Indigenous Americans, including the Wampanoag Nation who met the Pilgrims, have similar practices.

"We have been given the duty to live in balance and harmony with each other and all living beings. So now, we bring our minds together as one as we give greetings and thanks to each other as People."

The suggestion here is that we have the capacity to be something more than isolated individuals. We are also People. We are, or could be, forces of balance and harmony for each other and for other beings. How can this be? How can we be People in the largest sense? The practice of gratitude can help.

When we practice gratitude, we can't help but remember that we exist in relationship with the larger life around us. Experiment with noticing small, good things. Consider listing them: that way the tops of the trees look against the sky, a good cup of tea, a moment of ease. Notice that this noticing of things to be thankful for invites us to stop doing and start being. It turns out that just being still, bringing out attention to our present moment experience, returns us to a natural state of receptivity and connection.

There are many versions of the origins of Thanksgiving, including records from early settlers. As president of the United States, George Washington proclaimed the first nationwide Thanksgiving, marking November 26, 1789, "as a day of public thanksgiving and prayers." During the Civil War, Lincoln moved the date to November 21.

According to descendants of the Wampanoag Nation, the feast of thanksgiving began in an atmosphere of fear and not knowing. In their version of the story, in 1621, the Wampanoag heard the Pilgrims were firing off their guns and canons and thought it might be a declaration of war. Chief Massasoit and a party of warriors traveled to the Plymouth Colony to find out. They stayed for days, hunting and foraging and sharing food with the Pilgrims. There was no formal invitation to a shared feast on a set date. It arose in the midst of circumstances and it went on for quite a while.

Thanksgiving can take place in midst of an atmosphere of uncertainty and fear. Offering thanks doesn't have to happen just one day in November. The Mohawk Thanksgiving Greeting ends with giving

thanks to the Creator, or Great Spirit, the animating force in everything, and the source of "all the love that is still around us . . ."

As we learn to allow ourselves to be still with our pain, we may
discover a new spaciousness—an awareness beyond the thinking
mind that can just be without needing to name or to cling to or to
push away.

The practice begins with a simple movement of recollection—
both in the sense of remembering where we are, which is here, and
in the sense of collecting ourselves, being mindful of body, heart,
and mind.

On the night of his awakening, the Buddha faced terrible armies
conjured by the demon Mara. He didn't seek to banish them, nor to
lash out blindly. Instead, he reached down and touched the earth,
asking it to bear witness to his right to be sitting there. He knew that
even in the grip of his worst fear, the earth was with him. He knew
he was welcome. He sat there upright and open, experiencing his
breathing and witnessing everything inside and outside until he
achieved that state of clarity and calm and collection the Buddhists
call awakening.

In such a state we can't help but give thanks. We understand that
we live in a vast interconnected web of life, and that remembering is
not thinking about the past but a way of embracing all that is present.

How can we begin, especially if we are feeling lonely or afraid
or very sad? Make yourself available to life in small ways. Take a few
conscious breaths. Do some very small good thing, like smile at yourself in the mirror or smile at someone else who looks like they need
it. Allow yourself to be still with your sorrow or pain.

The Mohawk thanks to the Creator: "Everything we need to live
a good life is here on Mother Earth." This does not mean there is no
darkness. It means there is also light. We are the light.

7

A Good Start

"Is this the Dutch Village?" my friend Liz asked a New York City police officer who happened to be standing in front of a replica of a big Dutch windmill, its blades slowly turning against a bruised-looking sky.

"This is New Amsterdam," said the cop. His deadpan tone suggested that this should be obvious to us, given the fake windmill and the location, which was Bowling Green, the city's oldest park on the southern tip of Manhattan. We were standing on the site where, in 1626, Peter Minuit, the Dutch colonial governor, "bought" the island of Manhattan from the Lenape, the Indigenous Americans who lived here.

"Your ancestors really liked to shop," said my friend Liz.

"That's the stereotype about the Dutch colonists, that they were all about commerce," I said. "But my ancestors were terrible at it. They left this place, thinking it wouldn't be worth anything."

The policeman seemed as underwhelmed by the scene that faced us as we were. An article in the *New York Times* described it as a colonial village with "12 traditional houses, a windmill and a greenhouse." The "village" turned out to be a row of little kiosks with Ye Olde Dutch facades selling French fries, herring burgers, stroopwafel, little wooden shoes, and gouda cheese. There was indeed a greenhouse selling tulips and demonstrating flower arranging, and all the selling and demonstrating was being done by smiling people from the Netherlands. But still.

I had known it would be hokey. And yet I had pictured being able to step into damp little wooden cottages, replicas, certainly, but still proportioned in a way that would allow me to imagine what life was like for the first Dutch colonial settlers on the island of Manhattan. Among them, some of my ancestors. I stood looking around. A light mist shrouded the kiosks on the green and the towers of the Financial District that rose up all around us. The whole scene, including my naive assumptions, was very sad. I thought my ancestors were right to leave.

The event was sponsored by the Netherlands Board of Tourism and Trade to celebrate the four-hundredth anniversary of Henry Hudson's 1609 voyage on the *Half Moon* (*Halve Maen*) into New York Harbor and up the river that came to be named for him. The Lenape, of course, had already named it. They called it *Muhheakantuck*, or "the river that flows two ways" or "waters that are never still." I came down here because there was a question bubbling in me that could not be quelled.

Months before, during my father's last trip to visit me, my sister and I drove him to Hyde Park, the home of Franklin Delano Roosevelt, and the site of his presidential library. The president was buried in the rose garden. My father was a child of the Great Depression and a veteran of World War II, and we thought he would find this historical site moving. He did. But something unexpected happened.

It was a humid summer day, and my father, who was living with advanced COPD and emphysema, couldn't take the walking tour. Instead, he rode along in a golf cart driven by a park ranger as the tour proceeded, and I rode with him. We came to stop at a point on the grounds that had a sweeping view of fields sloping down to the Hudson River. The park ranger hopped out of the cart and gestured around, inviting us to consider the long history and lush prosperity of the Roosevelt family. They weren't rich like their neighbors the Vanderbilts, the ranger explained. But there was plenty of inherited wealth.

The earliest Roosevelt American ancestor was a Dutch farmer who owned a fifty-acre farm in New Amsterdam, in what is now Midtown Manhattan, around 1649. As the wealth of New York grew, so did the Roosevelt family wealth. They traded in dry goods, sugar, and real estate. The ranger flashed a broad smile. It was easy to become rich in America, if you came that early.

If you didn't come in chains, I thought.

"Isn't that about when our Dutch ancestors came?" I asked my father.

"Yes."

"Boy, it takes a special talent to come here as early as they did and stay as poor as they did."

My father beamed at me and roared with laughter. I thought it was funny, too. And I also took comfort in the fact. My ancestors stayed poor, which meant that there were things they didn't do, didn't it? Didn't trading in sugar mean having some connection to slavery? Wouldn't dealing in real estate mean pushing Indigenous Americans off their land?

My ancestors decided their little farms wouldn't be worth much and moved up the Hudson Valley and farther north, becoming part of a group that family lore called "Mohawk Dutch," ultimately establishing rocky little farms on the banks of the St. Lawrence River. It's as if my ancestors couldn't get far enough away from success as it was measured in the mercantile terms of the Dutch colonists.

But did that make them good or just not savvy? To be bad at a cruel system, to have no knack for accumulating property and wealth, this didn't make them wise. But it was something I took comfort in. Early accounts of Jesuit missionaries describe the shock and contempt Indigenous intellectuals expressed at the deceit and competitiveness of the early settlers. Benjamin Franklin and others recount the unwillingness of those taken captive by Native American tribes to return to a system based entirely on material gain and toil, utterly lacking in dignity and freedom, especially for women.

But even if my ancestors couldn't thrive in such a system—even though they were repelled by slavery—did this mean they were compassionate and wise? Some friends of mine can find refuge in their ancestors, taking strength and inspiration in their capacity to survive. But my ancestors? They amassed no wealth at the expense of others, committed no atrocities. But this didn't mean they couldn't still have been selfish or miserly, part of a culture that prized rugged individuality over care for the whole community. They knew how to farm the land and make things with their hands, and some of them knew how to navigate and sail. But they were nonetheless part of this system that sought to colonize and extract what they could for as little as they could.

The Bowling Green field where Peter Minuit met the Lenape was once their council ground, a place for group meetings and public debate. Accumulating evidence in many fields (recounted in books including David Graeber and David Wengrow's recent *The Dawn of Everything*) supports the view that the Indigenous Americans would have scoffed at the notion that anyone could "own" land. This was not because they were primordial woodland folk, innocent of the ways of European civilization, but because they had reasoned it through. Greed, including the form called miserliness, led to a loss of freedom and personal autonomy and dignity.

Certainly, the Indigenous inhabitants of this land had their own blind spots and conflicts and mistaken beliefs, but standing there on the green, the Financial District rising up around us, I found it easy to imagine the Lenape being repelled by the grasping and deceptiveness of Peter Minuit, buying Manhattan Island for sixty guilders worth of trade, which amounts to about $1,193 in 2020 U.S. dollars. He probably thought he was getting a steal.

I couldn't sleep the night after my friend and I visited the Dutch colonial village. I kept thinking about how imbalanced and driven the European colonists must have seemed to the Indigenous Americans. In his memoir *Memories, Dreams, Reflections*, Carl Jung describes an encounter with an elder named Mountain Lake in the Taos Pueblo in 1932.

> Chief Ochwiay Biano said, "See how cruel the whites look. Their lips are thin, their noses sharp, their faces furrowed and distorted by folds. Their eyes have a staring expression; they are always seeking something. What are they seeking? The whites always want something. They are always uneasy and restless. We do not know what they want. We do not understand them. We think they are all mad."
>
> Jung asked Chief Ochwiay Biano (which means Mountain Lake) why his people thought the whites were all mad.
>
> "They say that they think with their heads," he replied.
>
> "Why of course," Jung replied. "What do you think with?"
>
> "We think here," he said, indicating his heart.[7]

Our most precious inheritance is our humanity, I realized. But it is not just passively received. It is acquired as we learn to turn toward ourselves with curiosity and compassion, seeing what has been unconscious or rejected. Being fully human depends on discovering inside ourselves a state of awareness that is greater than our conditioning and inherited beliefs and reactive functioning.

Every year in Japan, the ancestors are remembered, and hungry ghosts are fed, in a ritual called Obon. I once experienced a Western

Soto Zen version of this practice, including among the hungry ghosts all those beings that society rejects and those parts of ourselves that we abandon or try to hide. All beings are heirs to their karma, taught the Buddha. We cannot escape our individual or collective past deeds.

But we can change the past. The root meaning of *heal* in English means "to make whole." Healing the past means being willing to see without looking away. We are more than what happens to us and more than what we have done out of ignorance or fear or grasping. We are also capable of compassionate awareness and wise understanding.

Recently, as I was visiting my daughter who lives in Europe, Russia invaded Ukraine. Invasion of another land for gain is not a relic of the past. What Buddhism calls the "three poisons" of greed, hatred, and delusion are still alive and causing immense suffering, now televised and live-streamed. A week after the Russian military invasion, my daughter and I went to see Picasso's masterpiece *Guernica*, which many consider to be the greatest anti war protest art ever created. A twenty-five-foot-long mural painted in thirty-five days in Paris, it is a masterpiece of compassionate awareness.

It was a cool evening in Madrid, and we stood in line outside the Museo Reina Sofia for a good while. My daughter fretted a little about the wait for my sake, and this touched me because it reminded me of being young and fretting over my mother during her first visit to me, newly grown up and worldly wise and wishing to care for her as she once cared for me. Looking out over the courtyard, it dawned on me that Alex and I, and everyone, also stood in a line of mothers and children stretching back and back to our earliest ancestors.

Picasso understood this lineage of caring, pushed into the background by history, by the deeds and misdeeds of men. *Guernica* is full of images of animal innocence and human goodness destroyed by an unspeakable act of violence. Picasso painted the mural after hearing about the 1937 bombing of Guernica, an ancient Basque town in northern Spain. He used a kind of house paint, specially formulated to have no gloss, and in only black, white, and gray, echoing newspaper photographs.

The Museo Reina Sofia once housed the first public hospital in Spain. Walking through the halls to the gallery where *Guernica* is exhibited, it is easy to imagine the sick and wounded on stretchers, their cries echoing through the halls. But *Guernica* brings a kind of stillness. It changes the atmosphere of the gallery where it is exhibited. *Pay attention,* it commands. *This really happened. Stop and see. Stop and feel.* Glimpsing this great work reminded me that to be fully human we must be willing to see and to feel.

Gray and black and white, featuring among other images a gored horse and bull, a dead soldier, and women screaming, including one holding her dead baby, flames—the mural feels like one gesture, one unified action of compassionate witnessing and artistic realization. Picasso captures the horror of war. The root definition of *compassion* is to "suffer with," and Picasso's feeling for the suffering inflicted on the Basque town of Guernica is unmistakable. And yet, just as apparent are his clarity, confidence, and consummate skill.

We stood in front of the artwork for a long time. I am not an art historian or a student of Picasso, nor is Alex, who often filled in historical context when we traveled together. But I felt very directly that the mural's power to hold the attention came from being a work of heart and body and mind. Awakening means waking up to our full humanity, our full capacity for being present. It means bearing witness to life, using all of our capacities. And it means sharing what we experience.

The bombing of Guernica was conducted by the Nazi air force with the approval of the Italian Fascists at the request of Spanish Nationalists. It lasted for three hours. The Nazis called the mission "tactical," disrupting a trade route used by the Republican forces in the Spanish Civil War. But most of the world branded it an act of terror.

Most of the men of Guernica were off fighting. The inhabitants of the town, as Picasso knew and immortalized, were mostly women and children and animals.

The monumental work toured the world, raising attention and funds for the Spanish Civil War. In 1939, Picasso loaned the work to New York's Museum of Modern Art for safekeeping. Picasso himself lived in Paris during the German occupation of World War II. A German officer once visited Picasso's apartment and saw a photograph of *Guernica*.

"Did you do that?" asked the officer.

"No, you did," said Picasso.

The artist decided that his masterpiece should stay in New York, until democracy in Spain was fully established. In the summer of 1981, just months before it was returned to Spain, my mother and I saw *Guernica* at the Museum of Modern Art in Manhattan. I had just moved into my first apartment, and she came to stay with me. I was thrilled at her visit, and I was determined to take good care of her. I wanted her to experience beautiful big-city things. But the impact of *Guernica* on both of us was beyond all my earnest hopes and imaginings. It brought us both to silence. Afterward, we had lunch in the museum dining room. I remember how summer light washed the room. There were irises on the tables. But we were still quiet. "War is terrible," my mother said at last. It wasn't the kind of thing she was given to saying.

In the Museo Reina Sofia, Alex peeled me away from *Guernica*. We found we were too full of it to look at anything else.

"I feel a little guilty," said Alex.

"Don't," I said.

"I don't feel like looking at the *Guernica* T-shirts in the gift shop, do you?"

"No. I don't think the T-shirt version would do the experience justice."

I felt that I had just glimpsed what "doing justice" can mean. It means bearing witness, and expressing this witness. You didn't have to like Picasso to feel the depth of his protest against those who sought to take life and freedom from people.

We emerged from the museum to find the museum square full of people and heavenly sounds. Blue-and-yellow banners and Ukrainian flags waved slowly in the night air and a chorus sang Mozart and Verdi for peace. The crowd joined in, holding up their phones like candles. meeting war with prayerful beauty.

There is so much pain and suffering in the world, I thought, watching and listening. But there is also so much creativity and courage and compassion, seeking to meet that suffering. All over the world, and in all times, there have been people who have behaved bravely and generously. In the midst of darkness, there is light.

After the exhibit, Alex led me to a little noodle restaurant on a side street, near our hotel. It was cool and a light rain started to fall, and bowls of noodle soup seemed just the thing. I looked at her across the table, my descendant, sharing the awareness that this was a small good thing to be doing, to be together and having soup in a world full of suffering and the struggle to overcome suffering. Small, but a good start.

Once I found a wallet on a train platform in Grand Central Station. Strangely, I was the only one in the crowd to notice it. People rushed along, boarding train cars; conductors stood by open doors. Nobody saw it. How could this be? It was as if everyone was in a trance except me. I had no choice but to pick it up. I settled in my seat, wondering what to do next.

Up until that point I had been savoring one of the great pleasures of New York or any walking city or town: public solitude. It was a pretty day, and I had walked back to the train station after lunch with friends. I loved the feeling of flowing along in a river of humanity, watching all manner of states of being pass by—rich and poor, joy and sorrow. But I also loved the feeling of doing this safely encased in my own little bubble of thought and observation.

Seeing the wallet lying on that busy platform unnoticed was shocking enough to burst my bubble. It woke me up to the strange reality that we are all doing the same thing—all of us floating along in our own bubbles, lost in our own stories, the center of our own tiny universes. It was a small shock, not an attack or a declaration of war, yet it awakened compassion in me and reminded me that I was also part of a shared world.

As an exercise, allow yourself to remember that part of the larger stream of life—that the pains you are experiencing are not yours alone to be hidden as if they are shameful, but part of "the" pain, our collective human pain—the pain of loss or rejection or not getting what you want. This experience reminds us that life isn't asking us to be superheroes, swooping in to perform great deeds. It is asking us to join in, to be available, to bear witness to what is happening and respond as kindly and wisely as we can in any given moment.

Looking through the lost wallet, I checked the driver's license and found it belonged to a young man, just twenty years old. He was carrying a bank card that belonged to his mother, based on the name, and a fair amount of cash. I felt a stab of sorrow for the young man, but then my heart lifted because I knew this would have a happy ending.

What to do? Should I walk through the car, looking for the young man myself? After a little consideration, I decided to take another leap into the stream of shared humanity. I let the conductor in on the situation. I showed him the driver's license and gave him the wallet. "This poor kid is probably looking very worried and scared," I told him. "And we can turn this around. We can give him evidence of the goodness of humanity." The conductor brightened and smiled.

Was I unwise to let go of that wallet and trust the conductor? It didn't cross my mind that I shouldn't. The exchange took place in the hearing of other passengers and no one called me crazy. He came back with a big smile on his face. He told me that he found the kid sitting one car back and gave his wallet back.

"He was *soooooo* happy," said the conductor, beaming. "All the people around him knew he had lost it, and all of them were happy, too."

This was one of those marvelous moments—and I've had several on trains—when people go from being alone to together, from solitude to community. The next time the conductor passed by collecting tickets he was humming. Everyone around seemed lifted up, looking at each other, released from their isolation.

The word *enthusiasm* comes from the Greek root *entheos*, "having the god within." There are moments when we feel we are flowing along with life, part of a greater wholeness, a greater story. The conductor, the young man, his supporters, me—a whole group of us were sharing something wonderful that didn't even need to be rendered in words.

Do you ever wonder what your purpose is? On Saturday, I saw that our purpose can change moment by moment. We are here to bear witness and to allow forces to pass through us—to return wallets, bring water to people who need it, to offer to be one more pair of hands on the bucket brigade in this burning world.

It is a small deed, playing a part in returning a dropped wallet, but for a moment I glimpsed what was really being accomplished, as effortless as breathing. How expansive and bright it felt to be part of the giving back of the wallet—as if I were joining the flow of life. How constricted and dark it would have felt to hold on to it, as if I were freezing life, binding myself, casting myself into darkness.

Almost at my stop, I walked back one car and introduced myself to Robert (that was the young man's name). He thanked me. We smiled.

"You made his day," said the lady sitting next to him.

"He made mine," I said. Just before I stepped off the car, I turned around. Robert smiled and waved—as did the lady next to him, and a few others who had witnessed the unfolding story of the wallet also smiled and waved. It sounds as if my commute on Metro-North had turned into an episode of *Mister Rogers' Neighborhood*. But this is what was also revealed: those who got on at later stops, who missed the wallet story, were sitting in their isolated bubbles.

Alone and together, in solitude and community, in one stream or another—this is the way our life goes. A wise man once told me to boil things down to seeing what is needed in any given moment. I've learned that what is needed is always first to remember that we belong here and that we are meant to flow.

May what I do flow from me like a river, no forcing and no holding back, the way it is with children.
—*RAINER MARIA RILKE*

8

My True Home Is Brooklyn

On the first night of my seven-year-old daughter Alexandra's first Buddhist retreat, Thich Nhat Hanh smiled and looked into her eyes as few adults ever look at children. Although he sat very still on a stage, the Vietnamese teacher seemed to bow to her inwardly, offering her his full presence and inviting her to be who she really is.

Alexandra threw her jacket over her head.

"Children look like flowers," said the man who was nominated for the Nobel Peace Prize by Martin Luther King Jr. in 1967. His voice was soft and bittersweet. "Their faces look like flowers, their eyes, their ears . . ."

Surrounded by scores of monks and nuns who had traveled with him from Plum Village, the French monastic community that had been his home since his peace activism caused his exile from Vietnam, he lifted his eyes from the little flower who was huddled, hiding her face, in the front row. Before him sat 1,200 people who had gathered in a vast white tent on the wooded campus of the Omega Institute for Holistic Studies in upstate New York. Thay, as he was affectionately known, had convened us for a five-day retreat dedicated to cultivating mindfulness through practices such as sitting meditation, walking, and sharing silent meals.

As the master talked about the "freshness," or openness and sensitivity of children, I couldn't help but be struck by the way Alexandra was ducking for cover. He extolled freshness as one of the qualities that each of us possesses in our essence, our Buddha-nature. Alexandra, shrouded in nylon, was reminding me that true freshness isn't limited to those moments when we feel happily and playfully open. It often means feeling raw and vulnerable. I wondered if it had been a mistake to bring her here, to risk exposing her to the way we really are.

During the retreat, children and adults came together during different parts of the day. In addition to sharing meals and a daily mindfulness walk, the children clustered at the front of the stage for the first twenty minutes of Thay's dharma talks, which he carefully framed in simple, poetic images that children could remember. I brought Alexandra hoping that contact with Buddhist practice would stimulate her imagination and awaken her own wisdom. I thought she could be inspired by the various techniques Thay described, such as listening to the sound of a bell that can call us back to "our true home."

"My true home is in Brooklyn," Alex whispered. She had peeled off her covering and lay stretched out on the floor with her head in my lap, jittering her foot to convey how bored and impatient she was. On the first night, most of the other children nearby were sitting cross-legged, quietly, and listening with what seemed to me preternatural attention. Alexandra was muttering to herself and writhing around on the floor like a big, unhappy baby. I wondered if she had some mild form of autism that had escaped detection.

Seventy-three-year-old Thich Nhat Hanh was sitting directly above me, embodying a mountain-like stability and compassion. A monk on the stage winked at Alexandra, a pretty young nun dimpled up in a fit of silent giggles. The people around me were friendly and relaxed. I felt like a terrible mother to be judging and comparing my daughter in these gentle conditions. It was almost as if the spirit of nonjudgmental acceptance that surrounded me was triggering a perverse reaction, drawing out my darkest, meanest thoughts. I felt like a vampire who had stepped out into the sunlight.

As we made our way back to our little cabin, the power went out all over the Omega campus. And a light turned on inside Alexandra. We stopped on the path, unsure which way to turn. I had left the flashlights behind. Alexandra took charge.

"Let's go back to the visitor's office," she said, leading the way. A kindly man on the Omega staff gave Alexandra a candle and walked us to our cabin.

"You knew just what to do," I said as I tucked Alexandra into bed. "That was good thinking."

"I hated to think of you wandering around in the dark," she said, beaming in the candlelight.

The next day Alexandra asked, "Mommy, is Thich Nhat Hanh a man? Like, does he have a penis?"

Yes, I offered, he was an ordinary man, but he was a monk. That meant that he lived for the happiness of others, so he might seem different.

My answer felt vague and wimpy, not as real as the question.

The following day in the dining hall, I discovered how deeply traveling with your own pint-size Zen master makes you feel aware of yourself, and how apart. The majority of the people there were moving about with a kind of underwater grace, practicing silence. We parents struggled with the task of filling trays and settling children while trying to remember to stop and breathe consciously when the mindfulness bell sounded.

Alexandra and I sat at a table in the dining hall facing a table decorated with pumpkins.

"Mommy!"

I whispered to her that we were supposed to try eating silently together.

"This is not my experiment," Alexandra reminded me. "I don't want to do it because I have a question."

"What's your question, Alexandra?"

"Is a pumpkin a fruit or a vegetable?"

"A vegetable."

"Why are you being so mean? Aren't you supposed to be happy?"

The interconnection of all phenomena was a constant theme of Thich Nhat Hanh's. He spoke often of "interbeing," the actual state of reality that, once recognized, nurtures compassion and empathy. As people ate in silence around us, I remembered an incident that had happened several weeks earlier. Alexandra was going through a phase of pondering how she was related to the first person who ever lived and to all other people.

"Every living being is connected," I had told her as I was putting her to bed one night. "The whole universe is alive, and what you put out in the world is what you get back. If you put out love and kindness, you tend to get love and kindness in return."

Alexandra and I had decided to put the little purple bike with training wheels that she had outgrown down on the street for someone to take. She crayoned a sign that read, "Whoever takes this bike, please enjoy it, love Alexandra."

She had been full of anticipation. The next morning she bolted out of bed and ran to the window.

"Mommy, my bike is gone!" she'd said, as radiant as on Christmas morning. "Somebody took my bike!"

The concept of the web of life was alive and breathing that morning. But by the end of the day, not surprisingly, she had moved past the shimmering magic and was applying the cause-and-effect practicality of a kid.

"So when do I get something back?" she asked.

David Dimmack, a longtime student of Thay's, was the volunteer in charge of the children's program on the retreat. He taught the kids the "Flower Fresh" song, the theme song of the Community of Mindful Living. At the beginning of a dharma talk one morning, they all got up on the stage together and sang to Thich Nhat Hanh and the rest of the sangha.

"*Breathing in, breathing out,*" sang Dimmack and the children.

"*I am blooming like a flower, I am fresh as the dew.*

"*I am solid as a mountain, I am firm as the earth. I am free.*"

When I stood in the back of the tent, watching the children onstage, it was impossible for me not to compare it to Sunday school.

Dimmack had called the songs "entertainment," matter-of-factly acknowledging that sometimes teaching just comes down to presenting ideas in a way that gently and gradually makes an impression, like water wearing away rock. At the same time, though, he emphasized that there was a constant creative tension in the children's program between teaching and allowing, between imposing structure and letting the kids be.

Mark Vette, another student of Thay's, works as an animal psychologist and lives on a ranch in New Zealand. Vette had the inspired idea of teaching the kids to use dowsing rods made of bent coat hangers and pendulums made of little pieces of wood.

"Here's the dowsing prayer," he said to the group of us gathering on a big meadow in the center of campus. "May I let go of the things that are known and embrace the things that are unknown." After the kids tired of looking for water and chasing each other ("Lead me to a dork!"), many of them settled down to find their place of "inner power." (The kids liked the word *power* better than *peace*.)

"Pendulums and dowsing rods seemed to be a perfect way to introduce them to their own intuitive sense," said Vette, a sandy-haired, athletic man who by the end of the week had completely captured my daughter's heart. "In the bush, these things work because we really already know where that lost animal is or where north is. And the kids can use it in the same way to learn to meditate, to find their center or their true home."

One day, during walking meditation, I began to get an inkling of what it is to find my true home. Every day the children, who left the dharma talk after the first twenty or thirty minutes, were invited to meet up with Thich Nhat Hanh and the grown-up students as they flowed out of the dharma hall to walk to the lake. On one beautiful azure day in late October, those of us who were with the children watched Thich Nhat Hanh walking toward us from the dharma tent, leading his multitude: 1,200 tall Americans dressed in bright Polartec colors following a small figure in brown.

No sooner had Alexandra and several other children joined to walk up front with Thay than she split to scamper off to the top of a leaf-carpeted hill.

"I'm going to roll down this hill!" she shouted to another girl. "Come on!"

It actually awed me that she was so unselfconscious about shattering the silence. Alexandra rolled down the hill, sounding like a bear crashing through a forest.

I dropped my head and trudged along. Suddenly, I noticed Thich Nhat Hanh gliding along, like a mountain on rails, almost next to me. His face looked calm and fresh, while mine ached like a clenched fist. Alex had raced ahead to the water's edge, where she stood waving and smiling at me. I felt a pang of love for her and really experienced how the voice of my heart was being drowned out by a welter of negative thoughts that seemed to come from somewhere in my brain that didn't even feel organic—more like a robot, a split-off part of me mechanically repeating bits of old programming.

Aware as I now felt, I was haranguing myself that really good mothers didn't get swamped by nasty reactions. Good mothers, my mind chided, were capable of unconditional love.

The bell calling for mindfulness sounded. I knelt down in the warm sand. The bell rang again, and a third time. I picked up my head to see an old man's hand gently stroking a familiar head of thick ash-blond hair. Thich Nhat Hanh and my daughter were sitting side by side. It slowly dawned on me that it was Alexandra who had just rung the bell calling the rest of us back to our true homes. Thay had been inspired to pick Alexandra, the loudest kid there that particular day, to sound, or "invite," the bell that called everyone to silence.

At that moment the ideal of unconditional love seemed nothing but a brittle concept, a fetter. I felt I finally comprehended what Thich Nhat Hanh meant when he said that acceptance is understanding and understanding is love.

"I was throwing sand, and I looked up and he was looking at me," she explained later. "He was kind of smiling. He waved for me to come over and sit by him. He didn't say anything; he just showed me how to ring the bell."

Back in Brooklyn, as Alexandra and I slipped back into our daily routines, I wondered from time to time what effect, if any, a week of mindfulness training might have. Then, one night many months later, I was fuming with frustration.

"Breathe, Mommy," said Alexandra. "Just relax and breathe and return to your true home."

Soon after he attained enlightenment, the Buddha went walking. He was probably delighted to stretch his legs because he had been sitting for a very long time (for forty days, according to legend, although scholars believe that this is not a literal number but an ancient expression that means "a very long time"). He walked without a fixed aim. Picture him taking in the world with new, enlightened eyes.

His radiance, his je ne sais quoi, was so striking that another man passing by stopped him in his tracks.

"What are you?" the man asked the Awakened One. "Are you a god?"

"No," the Buddha replied, probably with a serene smile.

"An angel?"

"No."

"Are you a wizard, then?"

"No."

"Are you a man?"

"No."

This last answer probably confounded the poor man. What was left? Wasn't the Buddha an ordinary human being like the rest of us? What changed after his enlightenment? It wasn't what he gained, but rather what he lost. The fear, craving, distraction you can see in most pairs of eyes—it was gone.

"I am awake," replied the Buddha.

The Awakened One was not a typical human being in the sense that he was free. This did not mean that he was free of all danger. This did not mean a snake would not be a snake. He did not ignorantly believe that it was just a stick. It meant that he was no longer at war with reality. He was not saying no to what is and yearning for some imagined better place or state where he could finally rest and say yes. He was all here, in body, heart, and mind. He was radiant with presence.

Bring attention home to your present moment experience, allowing yourself to be at ease. Just rest in kind awareness. Allow yourself to remember times and situations and beings with whom you felt completely relaxed and free to be yourself. This could be in nature, or with an animal companion or a loved one or a baby or a compassionate stranger. You might be playing or dancing or being still. Allow different occasions to appear. Remember moments of being in the presence of another being or in the invisible presence of nature or in the stillness of a special place—moments that felt radiant, when that attention made you feel wonderful and acceptable and free.

9

In the Midst of Winter

The night my daughter Alex put her bike out on our Brooklyn street for any stranger to take she lay in bed with her face shining with happy anticipation. Things appeared and disappeared on the street all the time, but it was different being part of it. In a way, this was what I wanted her to understand: Meaning is an action; we make meaning through our actions. You exist in a web of life: this was the message. You are part of nature and part of the human community. And when you give, you receive something.

A good friend of mine once told me that her father took her and the other kids in the family to Coney Island to look at the rides through a fence. To an adult, observing other people riding the Cyclone or the Wonder Wheel may have seemed a clever money-saving move, almost as good as the real thing or even preferable: people don't die watching roller coasters. To the children, of course, it wasn't even close.

Some truths must be lived. I knew this, even though I spent a lot of time reading and thinking about life. The aspiration for Alex, beyond recycling a little purple bike with training wheels that she had outgrown, was to kindle something inside her: an interest in the great exchange that is always happening in life and a sense of being part of it. I could barely find words for it, and I was far from being a role model of engagement. I was an overthinker, an observer. The hope was that if all the elements came together with the action in the street, the larger idea might take fire.

The next morning Alex clambered down the steps from her loft bed and flung open the drapes of the big windows in the living room. She whirled around, her face aglow. The bike was gone! We marveled together, although we were marveling at different things. I was marveling at having given birth to a child who seemed to take joy in giving without knowing who might benefit, who seemed to delight in being part of the dance of life. Incredibly, in spite of my own doubts and major flaws, I seemed to have pulled off something amazing.

"So when do I get something back?" she asked, her big eyes without guile. I had no answer. It was as if a curtain had been drawn back, revealing a blank wall. Alex was asking profound questions, and I shared them: Is the universe benevolent? How can we begin to understand our relationship to this life?

We can begin by noticing life just as it is. The thinking mind hates this kind of suggestion. It wants certainty. It wants to lift itself up above our flowing, changing, moment-by-moment experience, the world of the body and its perceptions and feelings. It wants us to be someone, and it wants life to be predictable and within our control. But our Brooklyn neighborhood gentrified, and our brownstone sold to a Wall Street investor and his young wife, who brought an architect into our apartment to discuss massive renovations as I sat at my desk, trying to work.

We moved to northern Westchester. Alexandra grieved for the life and diversity of Brooklyn, withdrawing into the world of *Harry Potter* and *The Lord of the Rings*, spending hours online with friends who shared her interests. I made a stab at gardening, hoping to soothe and ground us in our new life, to bring a happy little kid back to me by getting her in touch with the earth.

Stab is the correct word for the effort I made, brief and blunt. Only if a person were blind and drunk and working without tools could they get muddier than I even when I was just transplanting a few flowers. Reluctantly, Alex joined me a few times, wandering outside wearing rubber boots and pajama bottoms, trailing a trowel as if she were joining a chain gang.

Alex complained that everything about the digging and the planting went slowly. I told her that the work and the pace were the same for our earliest ancestors, but I knew this couldn't be true. They would have starved if they had farmed this way. Alex said she didn't like pretending we were "back in ancestral times." I didn't blame her. We were not our ancestors, and we couldn't know what they knew. There are truths that cannot be realized by outside observation, by superficial efforts, by quick stabs. What drove me to keep trying to teach what I didn't understand? I wanted Alex to feel welcome on the earth. I wanted to show her to be strong and have hope—not as a form of certainty but as an attitude of optimistic expectation. But it seemed we were all being swept along passively by time and circumstance.

Within the year, a superstorm flooded the downstairs and washed the garden beds away. I ran around the house in the middle of the night, on my way to the basement to save boxes of pictures and diplomas and other items. The seemingly solid ground turned to liquid mud. Some truths can only be experienced: the ground giving way beneath our feet is one.

Life is always in movement and always uncertain. Yet deeper truths are revealed when we need them; doors open from the inside. I learned this one December, in the international arrival terminal of JFK Airport in New York. It had been a long and difficult trip, and I pictured snuggling safely into the car and soon my own warm bed, a returning warrior battered but enriched by my experiences. I reached my hand into the bag and that bubble burst. Somewhere between the baggage claim and the car, my wallet had disappeared.

I took everything out of my bag and examined the interior, and then I did it again, unwilling to accept the gaping absence of something that felt so essential to my sense of security. I cycled through the expected reactions: panic and disbelief, the desperate hope that some honest citizen had turned the wallet in, then rage and self-blame about little things, that psychic cutting technique we use to ward off the greater pain of feeling vulnerable. I picked on little details. *Why did I stand in such a crowded place to retrieve my suitcase? Why didn't I wait?*

Home from the airport, after a flurry of phone calls, I lay in bed in the dark, wrestling with the dark angel of the deeper why. *Why was I so careless?* A chorus of witchlike voices chimed in: *You've always been this way.* I felt like a blind and wounded giant lurching around breaking things inside. *Why hadn't I gone ahead and bought that ridiculously expensive sweater or that expensive scotch or that age-reversing face cream I saw in the duty-free shop? It would have been better than just losing all that money to dark unseen forces, wouldn't it?* I was in no state to remember the night I had urged Alex to give her little purple bike to the universe, but the contrast was crazy. How could I trust in the goodness of life?

In spite of all of our care and precaution, life is unpredictable and subject to change. Our sense of security and control is mostly an illusion. No matter how hard we try to be safe and achieve and become someone sane and solid in this world, life is still unpredictable, and we are wavering creatures. Unexpected things will happen at unexpected moments. There will be pleasure and pain, gain and loss.

I lost the wallet during the darkest time of year in the Northern Hemisphere, days before the winter solstice, the day when the North Pole is tilted farthest from the sun. Our ancient ancestors noted that darkest day, watching the stars and noticing the shortening days, patiently abiding until one day there came a shift: the darkest day was followed by a little more light.

In Newgrange, in the east of Ireland, there is a mysterious Neolithic monument, a huge circular mound with a passageway and interior chambers. Tests reveal that it was built in 3200 B.C.E., which makes it older than both the pyramids in Giza and Stonehenge. No one can say exactly what it is for—a tomb, a place of rituals, something else entirely. But here is where it gets extraordinary: it was built so that the light of the rising sun on the winter solstice, on December 21, floods the chamber. Just as the sun rises, sunlight pours through an opening above the main entrance, shining along the passage and illuminating a carving of a triple spiral on the front wall.

I have often imagined how it must have been to gather in that chamber five thousand years ago, how dark it must have been before dawn in a world lit only by fire. Why did these ancient ancestors undertake such a vast and exacting project? Some researchers speculate that they were ritually capturing the sun on the shortest day, as if they were children capable of little more than magical thinking. But the engineering and astronomy required to build Newgrange refutes this. It is a monument to attention and faith.

Lying in bed the night of the wallet, finally exhausted from all my thinking, I considered this extraordinary feat. It seemed amazing to me that these ancient people could stay open and observing that way in all weather, going on being with life without rushing to conclusion. Left to its own devices, the ordinary thinking mind tends toward pessimism. *The light will never return*, it tells us; *it is always darkest before it is pitch black*: that kind of grim prediction.

A shift occurs when the thinking mind emerges from its self-enclosed isolation and reenters the world through the perceptions and feelings of the body. Most of the time we modern people treat the body as if it is little more than a mute animal that carries us around. We dress it and feed it and sometimes buy expensive moisturizer for the poor thing, but mostly it disappoints us, even as it tries to serve us as loyally as a good dog.

The trip that landed me in JFK had been a visit to my now-grown daughter Alex, educated, married, and living in England. How do these changes happen? Often during the trip, I looked at my jet-lagged face in the mirror, bewildered by what I saw: who was this older-looking woman with the vaguely worried look in her eyes? Most of us feel we are not enough somehow, not quick enough or somehow substantial enough. Life sweeps us along, and it often seems there is no solid ground.

In Buddhism, a definition of faith is the ability to keep our hearts open in the darkness of the unknown. The root of the word *patience* is a Latin verb for "suffer," which in the ancient sense meant to hold, not to grasp but to bear, to tolerate without pushing away. Being patient doesn't mean being passive. It means being attentive, willing to be available to what is happening, going on seeing and noticing how things change. When we aren't wishing for something to be over or freezing around an idea about what it is we are seeing, we see and hear more. We notice that nature has cycles, that each day is not the same length and quality, and that darkness passes.

We don't have the same close connection to nature that our ancient ancestors had, but we have the same bodies, hearts, and minds and the same capacity for attention with faith. The Buddha described the experience of enlightenment in many different ways. A Zen master once explained that enlightenment happens in small moments, many times. These moments tend to come when we stop fighting reality, when we relax and open. This state of opening is also called liberation, and it often comes in the midst of what we think of as failure and crushing disappointment.

We each find the deeper truths in our time and own way. We find them as we learn to observe from the inside. In England, my daughter and her husband drove me to visit the sets of the Harry Potter films. It was a pilgrimage to a modern Newgrange, a monument to the work that showed young Alex the magical potential of life, the way the light gets in no matter how dark. J. K. Rowling, author of the *Harry Potter* series, once told a Harvard graduating class that failure was the bedrock upon which she built her real life. Failing utterly by worldly standards granted her the freedom to strip her life down to the essentials, to tell the story of a lonely boy who, unknown to himself, was really a wizard.

Lying in bed that night, I remembered that the Buddha also believed he was a failure. Alone on a riverbank, split off from his yogi brothers, he broke his vows and took food offered by a young woman. Nourished by this simple act of kindness, he remembered a simple time from childhood. He had sat alone under a rose apple tree, watching his father and other men from his village plow the fields for spring planting. Peaceful and happy, with no adults bothering him, he could be open and attentive to life as it flowed around him.

The boy Buddha also saw insect families tossed about by the plowing and felt a pang of compassion. He took this impression of equanimity, of being open to the flow of life and to joy and sorrow and all that arises, under the bodhi tree. This memory of being kind and humble and selfless, just a little kid sitting under a tree, became the bedrock of his enlightenment.

At about 1 a.m. on the night I lost my wallet, the iPhone on the bedside table lit up. A band of light flashed across the screen in the dark, a message from my daughter in England. *Mom, I'm so sorry this happened to you.* In the light of day and in smooth times, such a message would be no big deal, just some nice words. But that night it was a candle in the darkness. The eye barely registers the light of a candle in broad daylight, but on a dark night it can be seen a long way, shining out as a reminder that there was still warmth and benevolence in the world, the possibility of companionship and kindness here in the midst of it all.

I felt a little blip of love and gratitude. I thanked her and another little message flashed back. It was a trifling exchange, complete with emoticons, yet it felt wiser and more alive than the dire and dramatic racket in my head. Once when she had been younger, I told my daughter that it was more important to be kind than to be right. Now I realized that kindness is also wise.

Lying in bed in the dark, watching my iPhone light up, it dawned on me that the meaning of life, the real purpose of our presence here, is being attentive, being willing to go on seeing and keeping our hearts open—not just for our sake but for the sake of others. We make ourselves available to life, opening our hearts to the passing flow of it, knowing we will blunder and get it wrong but sometimes right. We do this even knowing that those hearts will inevitably break because life is uncertainty and change and loss. But sometimes when we are open, light floods the darkest chamber.

> In the midst of winter, I found there was, within me, an invincible summer. And that makes me happy. For it says that no matter how hard the world pushes against me, within me, there's something stronger, something better, pushing right back.
>
> —ALBERT CAMUS

In dark times it can be a healing exercise to remember the stories of others who have gone through darkness and emerged into light. Please don't limit yourself to designated spiritual figures—the Buddha alone in the forest or Jesus wandering in the desert. Allow yourself to remember beloved stories and characters from books and films. Consider, for example, the deep truth in Charles Dickens's *A Christmas Carol*.[8]

In the course of one harrowing night of remembering, Scrooge moves from isolation to openness to life.

Scrooge, as most of us know, is a miserable, isolated man, "self-contained and solitary as an oyster." On Christmas Eve, he finds himself alone in a cold and gloomy house, dismissing the need we all have for warmth and human company as "humbug." He falls asleep, thinking only of the work he has to do. Enter the ghost of Scrooge's business partner Marley, wrapped in chains made of cashboxes and ledgers, the objects of his attention in life.

"You are fettered," says Scrooge, trembling. "Tell me why?"

"I wear the chain I forged in life," replies the Ghost. "I made it link by link, and yard by yard."

Marley warns Scrooge that he is forging his own chain and his will be even longer. In Buddhism, the fetters are mental bonds, habits of thought that limit us. Meditative awareness allows us to bring an accepting, nonjudging attention to all the ways we have learned to brace ourselves, seeing that these braces became postures and attitudes and finally beliefs. But Scrooge doesn't acknowledge this and rushes to defend the way his old partner is braced and bound. He reminds his old partner that he was "always a good man of business."

"Business!" cried the Ghost, wringing its hands again. "Mankind was my business. The common welfare was my business; charity, mercy, forbearance, and benevolence were, all, my business. The dealings of my trade were but a drop of water in the comprehensive ocean of my business."

Our real business here on earth is becoming more fully human, more aware and responsive. The details of our work . . . So many of us are taught to focus on achievement and accomplishments, tangible proof that we have done something singular that matters, that we are singular and we matter. But now more than ever, sequestered as we are, we begin to see that our real work may be seeing and feeling moment by moment, opening to a greater life.

Marley moans and shakes his chains, terrifying Scrooge with the spectacle of spending a whole brief life like that, bound up in hurt and anger and delusion, missing the possibility we have to open to life in a new way. What can possibly be done about this? How can we awaken?

We all have these frightening moments. We catch ourselves in the act of being caught up in this or that or after the fact. *Where did the time go? Why did I waste so much of it in this narrative or that?* In retrospect, we see ourselves trapped in delusion or aversion or craving something that turned out to be so not worth it.

Three more spirits come to Scrooge. These spirits bring moments of a deeper awareness of past, present, and future. Suddenly, Scrooge sees and feels what he usually misses, the poignancy and beauty of life, and he also feels how it is to be "squeezing, wrenching, grasping, scraping, clutching, covetous."

We long to see clearly and to be seen. Yet Marley's ghost and the other spirits convey how startling this can be. It is said that the Buddha could see peoples' past, present, and future—could view the source and the end of their suffering. Sometimes, when conditions are just right, we can see this way too. Such a gaze liberates. But it also burns because it awakens in us a feeling of the value of life. We notice that life passes so swiftly and that we miss quite a lot of it.

Before he leaves, Marley's ghost leads Scrooge to an open window where he sees "the air full of phantoms, wandering hither and thither in restless haste, and moaning as they went." They missed their chance to be really and truly alive while they were here.

Scrooge wakes up on Christmas morning and finds that it is not too late. He is overjoyed to discover he can live his life in an entirely new way. As an experiment, notice how it feels to imagine yourself beginning life anew. Notice how it feels to shift from old standards of achievement—amassing money or status or things—to qualities of heart and presence. Imagine how it would feel to measure your life in moments of openness and loving friendship and generosity.

10

Hessian Soldier

I stood on the street below my apartment on East 6th Street in Manhattan, waiting for an unmarked van to pick me up and drive me to an unknown location. I did know the person who contacted me, but in the interests of "scientific purity" I was told nothing about what I would be involved in, just that it would happen after dark—whatever "it" was—and that I should expect to be gone all night.

What was I doing? Not just on that night but in my life?

As it grew later, it grew brighter and louder in the East Village. Around the corner on Avenue A, a crowd gathered around the Pyramid Club, a punk-rock and drag nightclub. The cafés and art galleries on the block blazed with life. Allen Ginsberg lived in the neighborhood, and I sometimes meditated with him with a Tibetan Buddhist teacher at Philip Glass's house a few blocks away. *Wasn't that enough excitement and exploration? Did I really need to get in an unmarked van?*

I had moved from an apartment in a quiet neighborhood on the Upper West Side to this wild neighborhood. I gave up a job in publishing to be a freelance writer in a tenement apartment in the middle of a hipster carnival. I stood waiting, wondering at the way I put myself in situations where I thought the lightning of inspiration and insight might strike. Was this how a person woke up? I stood there, aware that I, myself, was part of the unknown in this equation.

The person who invited me on this mysterious mission was Michaeleen Maher, a paranormal researcher I had interviewed for a long magazine article about ghosts and the modern-day scientists who try to prove their existence. She told me that my story had drawn the attention of the producers of a television show called *Unsolved Mysteries*, and they had invited her to conduct an experiment in a legendary haunted location, which would later be reenacted in an episode of the TV show.

There is a myth that throwing a piece of pasta against a wall will tell you if it is cooked to the right degree. This always struck me as a silly way to cook, but I found myself doing something similar with my life. I was throwing myself at things to see what might hold me. I had no idea about what I was doing or what would happen. But I was open. I yearned to sink beneath the shallow and repetitive thoughts that went round and round, the anxieties and expectations. I wanted to live deep. I wanted to feel that I belonged to life. A white van pulled up; a door slid open; and a real-life ghostbuster beckoned me in.

I had first met Maher in an elegant apartment on Washington Square, the scene of one of her more memorable investigations. This was where Kathleen (not her real name) had frozen at the sight of a hunched-over figure in a black robe and her mother had watched a transparent black form passing down the hallway the following night. Maher had brought in a team of volunteers with a Geiger counter, infrared photography, and other equipment to investigate.

While riding in the van toward the unknown location, I learned that I was to be part of a new experiment. There would be no Geiger counters or photography this time, but a mix of psychics and skeptics who would be led through an old inn that was legendary for haunting activity. I was designated a skeptic and told I would serve as a control in the experiment because my article came to the conclusion that these kinds of investigations of ghostly events can offer no clear scientific proof, just hints and stories. Although I didn't say so, being labeled a skeptic hurt my feelings.

Finally we arrived in Merion, Pennsylvania, and the General Wayne Inn (as described earlier), which was established in 1704. George Washington slept there, as did William Penn, Benjamin Franklin, and the Revolutionary War hero General "Mad Anthony" Wayne (and the inn was renamed in his honor in 1793). Edgar Allan Poe drank (heavily) at the inn and wrote parts of *The Raven* there. In 1843, he also carved his initials in one of the windowsills.

Dark and heavy and sad—this was my impression of the inn after hours. Even if it wasn't haunted, it didn't feel like a place where happy things happened. For a long time this seemed to be so. A dozen years after my visit, a subsequent owner of the inn was found dead in his office, murdered by his business partner. The suicide of the murderer's girlfriend followed.

The Buddhist tradition describes "happy destinations"—including various heavens and this earth—and "evil destinations"—places of unbroken suffering. The inn was treated as an evil one and shuttered until 2005, when it became a synagogue and community center. When I learned this, I wondered if the Jewish congregation thought they could liberate with prayer the spirits that shadowed the place.

But that night, we were there to investigate the ghostly sightings and events that had been reported by many people over many years. Among the possible spirits, including a lost little boy and two servant girls caught stealing, there were reports of a Hessian soldier, and possibly more than one. And my job, it turned out, was to sit in a dark cellar all night, as the psychics were led through the inn one by one, starting in the attic.

I sat very still in the dark, marveling again that my life had come to this. I had friends who were doing concrete things to serve the world, building houses and healing the sick, and here I sat in a dark cellar, wondering if I was near (or maybe on) a ghost. The sheer weirdness of the situation invited intense self-examination.

With nothing outside to see, it was easier to see inside, especially the shallowness and repetitiveness of my ordinary thinking. As I waited in the dark, just breathing and sensing my body, I held a question that didn't even need words. *Who was I?* What on earth was I meant to be doing, not just in this cellar but in my life?

One by one, the psychics and skeptics were led through the building like bloodhounds. They would wander around, pausing here and there, and then leave. Finally the last one, the most celebrated of the group, stood stock-still with her back to me and gasped, reporting that she glimpsed a soldier in a green coat crouching in the corner. She was visibly shaken.

"I feel so much sadness and fear," she told me, holding herself as if she were cold. "So much sadness and fear."

She was sensing the presence of the Hessian soldier.

In American lore Hessians are thought of as brutal mercenaries, but these men were actually auxiliary troops of the British army, called Hessian because 65 percent of them came from the Hesse region around modern-day Frankfurt. The German prince who contracted them out to Great Britain profited handsomely, unlike the men themselves, who collected meager wages. The prince also collected blood money for every soldier lost. He called these unfortunate men his "Peru," comparing their value to the blood-soaked treasure the Spanish plundered from the Indigenous cultures of South America.

Far from being ruthless, they were extraordinarily disciplined and capable. Even George Washington had kind things to say about them, writing that they were more humane in battle than the British. The bad rap they eventually got came from the British themselves and, of course, from the American author Washington Irving, who created the Headless Horseman in *The Legend of Sleepy Hollow*.

Some Hessian soldiers were kidnapped into service. Among those unwilling soldiers were wayward students or young men with jobs that were deemed not important enough to keep them home. Had I been born a man in a different era, I was exactly the type who would have been a candidate for kidnapping. I could have been this ghost, crouching in this basement. My heart opened to this unknown being, trapped between two worlds. It was the subtlest inner movement. I was paying attention to my own experience, and then I noticed that I was noticing him. "Real" or not, for hundreds of years, he had been trapped here, not belonging to this world.

What is a ghost anyway? In the course of researching my article about ghost hunters, I had visited Karlis Osis at the American Society for Psychical Research, housed in an old brownstone on the Upper West Side of Manhattan. Born in Riga, Latvia, in 1917, Osis was a parapsychologist with a doctoral degree in the subject from the University of Munich. Tall and ascetic-looking, with a soft voice and a Latvian accent that made his words sound like spooky echoes rolling out of a cave, Osis told me that spending his youth surrounded by the devastation of World War I had inspired his interest in realms of awareness beyond what we can see.

There was also an indelible personal experience. As an adolescent lying in bed with tuberculosis, Osis had suddenly seen his room fill with a joyful white light. At precisely that moment, he later learned, his aunt had died. Osis went on to conduct ESP research at the parapsychology laboratory at Duke University, as a colleague of one of the famous figures of parapsychology, Dr. J. B. Rhine. But he never forgot that glimpse of white light, and he became certain that the greatest discoveries were to be found outside the lab.

Osis conducted a major survey of the deathbed observations of physicians and nurses in India and the United States, resulting in a book, *At the Hour of Death*. He told me that research also turned up evidence for the reality of ghosts. This was the phrase that Osis used in our interview that haunted me: Osis called ghosts "transit disasters."

For ghosts there is no release in a joyous burst of light, no liberation from the lonely isolation. Osis told me that ghosts are "exceedingly self-centered." Many living people are like this, of course, but as long as they are alive, there is the possibility that they will awaken. Ghosts are lost in a dream they can't wake up from; they look but cannot see.

In the Buddhist tradition, as well as other spiritual traditions, the human world is considered a place of special possibility precisely because we are positioned between heaven and hell. Each human life inevitably contains a mix of happiness and misery, and nothing stays the same. Things are lost without warning. Mishaps are always happening. Keys and jobs and great loves are lost, as well as a red wine spilling on a white suit. And it turns out that our true awakening depends on this very instability. It is in the midst of those awful moments that something inside us sometimes opens to a greater sense of belonging.

Being in a human body offers us the chance to take a very special kind of journey—from self-enclosed separation from others and the whole of life to a sense of belonging. On earth, we can all be heroes—not in the sense of being solitary actors brandishing swords, but by daring to put down our defenses and take off the armor to really experience and feel what is happening in any given moment, without fighting or fleeing.

Heroism can be a momentary action that happens on the inside without anyone else knowing. It is a movement of availability, of softening, of letting down our guard, and opening to life. What we discover then is that life is always new and surprising. We discover in those moments that it is not the old world of our known stories and ideas that will save us. It is our brave willingness to open to connect.

Under every other longing, we long to belong—to a group, to ourselves, to life itself. *Belonging* comes from the Old English root word *lang*, which means "having a great linear extent." It has the same root in Old Frisian and Old Saxon and Old High German. The ancient root also meant "drawn out in duration"—in the sense of "I have been here or I have been at this or that a long time." But the root also points to a depth and abundance the poor Hessian soldier couldn't have.

Opening to life, even for a moment, we realize our connection. The root of the word *compassion* means "to suffer with." Yet in the midst of suffering, we also remember the warmth of life. We remember, if only for a moment, the goodness of being alive, that in spite of everything there is love and compassion and possibility woven through it like psyllium. When we feel compassion, we remember that we are not alone.

Even if we don't believe in ghosts or in cosmologies that portray heavens and hells, we know how it feels to be stuck, to be caught in an isolated and isolating loop of thought that ancient Buddhists would call "a plane of misery." Innately, we understand that once you have landed in hell, it is very difficult to get out.

The Buddhist tradition teaches that if a yoke with a single hole was floating at random on the sea, and a blind turtle living in the sea were to surface once every hundred years—the likelihood of the turtle pushing his neck through the hole in the yoke would be greater than that of a being in the evil destinations regaining human status.

Sitting in the cellar that night, I began to understand being a human being isn't a thing, but a special state of openness. As gently and easily as it came, I understood that this openness could also be lost. For a long time, I used to think that staying human in this way involved a careful policing of thought. Negative thoughts were to be seen and nipped in the bud, or uprooted and replaced with positive thoughts. I pictured a prison matron sweeping the cell of my heart and mind with a flashlight, perhaps smiling softly and wrapped in a meditation shawl, but still a guard, ready to punish transgressions.

Over the years, I began to understand the importance of self-compassion. I began to see that as I accept painful thoughts and feelings, directly experiencing how closed I can be, a softening and opening begins to come. As I do this, I begin to notice that things can change. An idea or feeling that seems fixed and permanent is observed to have passed. Observing this is opening to a truth that is greater than any thought.

When I had sat with Kathleen and the parapsychologist in the kitchen of that apartment on Washington Square, we studied the infrared photo taken at the site with the parabolic arc of fog. They pointed out a dark circle that looked to me a little like the black-and-white teardrops in the interlocking yin-yang symbol.

"To me it looks like a face, a black face up close to the camera," said Kathleen.

Years later, I discovered that in 1819, an enslaved woman named Rose Butler was hanged, not in the elm tree across from the apartment, but on a gallows nearby for attempting to burn down the building of her enslavers. Had the gracious apartment I visited once been the home of those people? Had I glimpsed Rose Butler's face?

There are events that freeze us in time, split us off from our true selves. These traumas happen not just to individuals, but to groups of people and whole nations. Healing can take a long time. But it can begin, perhaps, with a willingness to just sit in the dark and open our hearts.

At a certain point in his great story, the man who would become the Buddha gave up all his great efforts. He went off by himself and remembered a time in early childhood when he was also by himself in nature. According to the story, the little boy saw some insects whose homes were being torn up, with loved ones lost due to the men of his village plowing the fields. His head wasn't full of solutions. The boy just sat there, secluded yet deeply connected to this life. His heart opened, and he felt compassion. This is the place to begin, the Man Who Would Wake Up thought. Just noticing what we don't usually notice, making space for what is beneath the surface, and allowing our hearts to open to it—this is the beginning of freedom for us all.

At times, everyone faces the darkness of the unknown. Practicing presence can help us connect to our personal power.

Once at the Rubin Museum I was asked to talk about power— and not just power but a specific embodiment of power. The image that was to illuminate my talk featured the Fifth Dalai Lama of Tibet, who unified Tibet in the seventeenth century and was revered for his temporal and spiritual wisdom and power. How could I relate to this? I decided that I could start by unifying myself.

The root meaning of *integrity* is "to be whole or complete or unified." This wholeness appears as we remember to be present— emerging from the isolation of thinking and remembering that we have a body and sense perceptions and a heart and feelings. As we ground and open to our present moment experience, we can set an intention. Before you begin any project or task, allow yourself to be present, to remember or re-collect yourself—and then set an intention to be sincere. Notice that this is not striving, but instead touching the earth of your life. *Sincere* comes from a Latin root that means "clean, pure or genuine"—not mixed with other stuff. The wisest intention is to be sincere, to go for the truth.

Intention comes from a Latin root that means "stretch." Allow yourself to envision this not as projection, but as making a journey, guided by the light of your own sincerity. To be sure, there was some stretching to be done to connect my living experience of the present moment to the Fifth Dalai Lama and seventeenth-century Tibet. I read about the unification of Tibet, and about the installation of the

Dalai Lama. I learned about magical powers in Buddhism—about the qualities that were believed to lead to the ability to fly, walk on water or through mountains, and appear in multiple places at once. And then I recalled that the Zen master Thich Nhat Hanh once said: "The real miracle is to walk on the earth."

He meant being *fully aware* of walking upon the earth, under the sun, alive in a mysterious universe. Personal power also has to do with unification, I realized. Awareness gains depth and dimension—becomes true presence—as we learn to be present in body, heart, and mind. It is only when we are fully present that we can truly see where we are and sense our connection to life. It is only then that we can see what is needed.

While I was preparing to teach at the Rubin Museum, I recalled a cartoon in the *New Yorker*. A raggedy young man stood with hands grasped around a sword in a stone. Merlin, great sorcerer and teacher, stands beside him. Many had tried and many failed to extract Excalibur, the magical blade that would empower a king and grant sovereignty over Britain. "Use thy core," says Merlin.

According to Arthurian legend that sword was magical and would be released from the stone only to one fit to rule. But it is also very possible that what made Arthur fit to unify his country was indeed his use of his core—his willingness and ability to come from the center of his being. His special power may have been his unified presence. With that in mind, I crafted an exercise for cultivating wholeness and unified presence that I called C.O.R.E. I knew this was a stretch, but a stretch in the sense of the root meaning of *intention*. The practice of C.O.R.E.—and of all spiritual practice—invites us to unfold, discovering that our true nature is mysterious and marvelous beyond measure.

C stands for concentrate. This does not mean mental strain or a narrowing of mental focus, but settling down and bringing the attention home to the body, to our present moment experience. Concentration is allowing the attention itself to settle us and collect us.

When we bring the mind to the body and the body to the mind, when we are more collected, our experience becomes more pliant and lighter. Bringing the attention to the breath can help in the concentration process.

O stands for open. When we sit down to be still and concentrated, we open to the life inside and outside us. It's a wonderful paradox that when we grow still, when we bring our attention home to the breath and our present moment experience, we don't shut out life. We open to it. We notice it and sense it. Opening is manifesting a wish or desire to live a greater life—right here and right now.

R stands for recollect or remember. *Sati*, the ancient term for mindfulness in Buddhism, means "to remember the present moment." We gather our disparate parts—head, heart, and body. When these parts touch, a new possibility appears. When we are recollected, we can investigate and understand our experience in a way we just can't with thinking alone.

E stands for embrace. When we are more concentrated and grounded, more open and clear, we can accept what is happening. This doesn't mean that we have to like it, but we can be present with it, investigating what is happening or what we are feeling with loving awareness. Grounded and open, we observe that life is constantly entering us and leaving us—as air and food as well as impressions and information of all kinds. We remember that even when everything seems to be going awry, there is a force of love. This is not a romantic attraction or attachment, but an energy and way of seeing that reminds us, always, that we are not separate from life. We are not strangers here, no matter how dark it seems. And we are meant to connect.

PART THREE

Mind

Before his full awakening, the Buddha sat meditating, watching his passing thoughts and emotions, which Buddhists call "mind states." He noticed that negative thought streams and mind states are like pirates, hijacking the ship of our good aims and intentions and leading us to dark little ports. Other thoughts and emotions fueled his aspiration to awaken. Yet he saw that all of his passing thoughts and states, observed with an attention that is free from attachment, could lead to deeper truths.

11

Speechless

One morning I woke up with no voice. I was left with just a faint, breathy whisper. This would be upsetting anytime, but on this particular day it felt as if I were in a fairy tale. In a matter of hours, I was supposed to tell a story and teach mindfulness meditation at the Rubin Museum of Art in Manhattan. And I couldn't make a sound.

In the middle of the working day, in a softly lit theater in a museum in New York, more than a hundred people of different ages, genders, and realities were going to sit down and be still together. The stories and guidance I wanted to offer were simple: I wanted to help them remember that they were alive.

Sati, the Pali word for mindfulness, literally means "to remember the present moment." During meditation, I periodically reminded everyone to return to the sensation of breathing, to notice when they were lost in thought and to come home to the direct experience of being in a body. The Latin root of *conspire* means "to breathe together." I loved reminding people that we were conspiring. And it did feel as if we were part of a radical movement, peeling ourselves away from our computer screens for a time to return to the roots of being.

Hiding under the covers, I tried talking, whispering, croaking, anything. Nothing came out, just a ghostly whoosh of air. Canceling was an option, but the event was new and it was doubtful that a replacement teacher could be found on such short notice.

Standing up did not help. Neither did stretching or walking or smiling bravely in the bathroom mirror. I padded through a quiet house awash in golden summer light. Terrible images flashed before my eyes: Faces looking up at me, uncomprehending, dismayed. People heading for the exits.

Once the Buddha taught without speaking, holding up a single white flower. That wordless gesture must have stunned a crowd who came expecting brilliant stories and answers to their deepest questions. Yet according to legend, nobody threw rocks or heckled the Awakened One, and one man understood that he was embodying the inexpressible suchness of life. But I was not the Buddha. There was no holding up a rose or a carnation purchased at a New York deli somewhere between Grand Central Terminal and the museum on West 17th Street. Someone might think it was a game of Buddhist charades and call out "Flower Sermon," which is what that teaching came to be known as. But no one was coming to the museum at lunch hour for an imitation. They were hoping for something real.

I stood on the stone floor of my front porch, looking through the screen door at the flowers and trees. Everything appeared still and serene, as if life were stable and predictable. But everything is subject to change. The flowers and even the bluestone slabs I stood on had not been here the year before, when I was not yet teaching at the Rubin Museum and had not yet been diagnosed with an essential voice tremor (after an initial misdiagnosis), a neurological disorder that makes my voice soft and husky at times, quivery at others.

After resisting for a while, I now undergo the standard therapy of injections of botulinum toxin in the vocal cords every three or four months. It helps. But the results can be unpredictable. A low dose that has worked well can become ineffective or suddenly too powerful, stealing a voice for many weeks.

"Maybe the universe is trying to tell you something," someone said to me, when I explained about my voice. This was not kind, but also not wrong. Being without a voice in a wordy world is oppressive, I learned. But not speaking can also help you listen deeply and observe.

During the difficult stretches, I saw that life rolled along perfectly well without most of my opinions, which are mostly shallow and secondhand, not worth the effort it takes to rasp them out. When it's hard to be heard, you need to mean what you say. Words need to be rooted in presence, in the real-time experience of how it feels to be here.

Life is difficult for everyone, I reminded myself. Even beautiful people with every seeming advantage live like combat soldiers much of the time—fighting for survival, struggling to maintain a positive attitude, wary and weary and scared. The people who were going to be filing into the museum were all fighting battles. They were seeking safety and welcome and company.

For brief periods, when life breaks our way, it can feel as if we are finally getting somewhere. We may think that we are finally becoming someone who understands this crazy life. With this self-image securely in place, we may decide that we are good and life is good and that we can share this with others. But things change. A voice or relationship or job or health is lost.

Instantly we contract, closing the doors and windows to intruders. We become little fortresses in a world that is suddenly dark and dangerous. I once heard a Buddhist teacher call the ego a defense against pain. I heard another great teacher say there is no point in trying to kill the ego because it was never really alive; it is a set of conditioned responses and thoughts that try to protect us by separating us from the whole. But we don't like living in these self-enclosed little air locks. We feel cut off from life. We are afraid to step outside. We want the comfort of the known.

I showered and dressed to go, frightened and worried about how I would come across on stage and what people would think about me. But within this feeling of being trapped in the spotlight, there was another discovery: That under this agitated mind there is another mind, vastly quieter and more responsive, seeing without judgment. And within the body that was so quirky and problematic, there was a subtler body, also receptive and responsive. In times of crisis, I remembered, this body knows what needs to be done. I got in the car and drove to the train.

Meditation and spiritual practice have been called death in life. We die to the hope that our life is taking us somewhere. We let go and allow ourselves to open to a new life, a shared life. I reminded myself that this happens with each breath, the letting go and breathing in. For the space of a few breaths, I escaped the diving bell of ego and looked at the brilliant blue sky.

I would have died if I hadn't died. This is a mantra I often share with others. I attribute it to the Danish philosopher Søren Kierkegaard, although it isn't an exact quote. It came to light in a college class discussion on Kierkegaard's leap of faith. After all these years, I'm not sure who said it just that way, if Kierkegaard said it or a professor or this was my own paraphrase. But the phrase stuck, and I made it my own over the years. Over and over, I verified that it is often when the worst happens, when hopes and dreams are dashed, that real life pours in.

I boarded the train. On this morning, it felt like more than a trip down to the city, but rather a journey. Still in the uppermost layer of my mind, the part that reasoned and compared, I judged as ridiculous this feeling of questing and yearning. There was no grand story unfolding and no role of a heroic individual. Things were just happening.

At a level of awareness deeper in my body, however, closer to what the ancient ones called soul or essence, there was a quest. *Who was I really? And what kind of life did I want to live?* Suddenly, these questions felt essential. In his Nobel Prize acceptance speech, the Irish poet Seamus Heaney said that we are all hunters and gatherers of values. I longed to live in a world that was bigger than my own little ego, to care about something more vital than sounding good or looking good, because that effort was doomed. It was meaning I was seeking, and for a moment I knew this wasn't a proposition that could be rendered in words. It was a feeling of being alive, part of a greater whole.

"We all have to be the hero of one story—our own," wrote P. L. Travers, the author of the Mary Poppins novels, in the first issue of the magazine *Parabola*, "The Hero."[9] But must we? When I first read this quote, I felt scolded by the magical British nanny for having a bad attitude, especially because Joseph Campbell, who popularized the hero's journey, was also a contributor to *Parabola*.

But now I understood that a hero is someone who can take off the armor, who can be vulnerable and show up anyway, experiencing what is really happening without trying to resist or run away. I saw that an act of heroism can be an action that happens on the inside without anyone else noticing, a movement of availability, a willingness to be seen and heard and touched by life.

All the way down to Grand Central Station, the fear and the sense of contraction that came with it hit me in waves. I noticed that when I thought about myself and what might happen, I suffered. When I stopped and noticed the people around me, I felt energized and alive. The fear was still present, but I remembered that I was also part of a larger life that contained unknown possibilities.

A hero's journey isn't necessarily a long ordeal. At any given moment, we can leave the self-enclosed world of our thought and touch down in the present moment, which is always unknown territory. Yet it also feels like coming home. It seems miraculous to move from one state of being to another, from thinking to opening to presence.

I walked the twenty-five blocks to the Rubin. At times, I felt like Anne Boleyn mounting the steps to her execution. But at the museum I was met by kindness. A glass of water and a cup of tea were fetched. A powerful hand microphone was supplied. When I first whispered to the crowd, there were a few murmurs of surprise and concern, not unkind. I told people to lean in, as if I were on my deathbed and about to tell them the secret of life, and they did. All but one person stayed.

Afterward, more than one person assured me they could hear me very clearly. Partly, this was due to the excellent sound system. But it was also because of the way they listened. Several people told me they were more touched by my willingness to show up and use my voice as it was than by anything I might have said under other circumstances.

That day I spoke about the great myth of the Buddha's journey to awakening, and especially about a time when he was overwhelmed by terrifying projections about what might happen to him. As he sat meditating under the bodhi tree, the devil Mara sent temptations to scare him into giving up his seat and his deepest search. Mara conjured images of the Buddha as a great leader, as immensely wealthy and powerful, surrounded by beautiful women. But the Buddha would not move.

When temptation didn't work, Mara resorted to fear, conjuring visions of terrible armies and horrible carnage. Still, the Buddha did not flinch. Slowly and wordlessly, he reached down and touched the earth. The classical explanation is that he was asking the earth to bear witness to his right to sit there, affirming his many lifetimes of effort to awaken.

But touching the earth also symbolizes humility, the act of coming down out of our thoughts to remember the body and the present moment, leaving the frantic control center of ego to join the rest of life. The Latin word *humus*, "the living earth," is related to the word *humility*. When great difficulty arises, we tend to remember that what really matters are essential, earthy things, giving and receiving a glass of water, a cup of tea, taking the next breath. It is during the hard times that we notice that life is constantly offering itself to us.

The meditation taught at the Rubin is always secular, accessible to all who enter. But on a big screen behind the stage where the meditation teachers sit there are projected images of sacred Buddhist art from the museum's collection. Among them are works featuring Padmasambhava, the "Lotus-Born," a Buddhist master of the eighth century. In Tibetan Buddhism, it is believed that this great guru had the power to foresee the future, hiding teachings to be discovered in years to come. He predicted an age of darkness, a time of great discord and destruction, when people would lose their ability to discern what is precious and what is mere distraction, sweeping them away from what is good and essential.

The great Zen sage Dogen taught that whenever people sit down to practice stillness, they sit down with the Buddha and all the ancient ones who have sought to awaken, including Padmasambhava, who is also called "the second Buddha." That day at the Rubin, in the midst of a dark time, I discovered that a truth was waiting to be found: When we let go and die to the known, we find the unknown. And when we dare to be still and to touch the earth of our lives, we can find our true voice.

The accident happened at the worst possible moment, although there is probably never a really good moment for a car accident. I was driving home through the rain, thinking about how much I had to do before I left for my daughter's college graduation that week. I was thinking about what a difficult week it had been and feeling triumphant. *I accomplished so much! Good for me!* And then . . . crash! I was driving through an intersection, almost home, when an elderly man turned left and smashed into me, demolishing the front of my car.

Time slows down during accidents and emergencies. A crystalline clarity comes. I was aware of my thoughts. *Wasn't I driving straight through a green light? Was the driver impaired? He turned on red!* But the thoughts seemed slow and overly simple, like a headline news stream compared to the full feeling of the impact. There was the sensation of the collision and the sound of crunching metal and breaking glass. And there was a deeper seeing. I watched myself try to refuse to take in what was happening. My mind tried to push it away with objections: *It wasn't right! Why did it have to be happening on the week of Alex's graduation? Why did I have to be in that place at that time?* And at the same time, a deeper awareness watched all this and more: I saw that every cell of my being was bracing itself, contracting, scooting away, *DID NOT WANT THIS TO BE HAPPENING.*

But all my thinking and objecting couldn't undo it. I sat stunned in the rain in my crushed little hybrid car. And it got worse. The other driver, an elderly man who did seem a bit disoriented, got out of the big van he was driving and yelled at me to call the police because he did not have a phone. His hit crushed my car and then he yelled at me! His bullying manner was so unexpected and so wrong that I burst into tears. A volunteer fireman appeared out of nowhere and slipped into the seat beside me. He asked me if I was hurt. I told him that I was not although my feelings were very hurt. He nodded, this witnessing angel. I told him that my daughter was graduating from college that week. I told him that I loved my little Prius and that I had just bought it a few months ago. I told him it had been a very difficult week. These things happen, he told me kindly. This seemed incredibly true and profound. A very similar thing happened to him not long ago, he continued. Someone was texting and ran into him. Accidents happen. We both nodded. The important thing was that no one was hurt.

People should pay attention, I told him, realizing in my shocked state that I was saying something deeply true. Being present helps a person not be hurt. Awareness is a kind of spiritual airbag, surrounding a person with compassionate witness, represented at that moment by the kind man beside me. We waited together in the rain for a long time until the local police came. I was amazed by his patience, and also amazed that I rarely think of patience as a spiritual quality.

The press of errands and tasks that had been consuming me just stopped. Traffic flowed on around us. I marveled that the drivers were as I had been, lost in thought. These thought worlds that we create are like waking dreams, holographic projections, I realized. We cannot control reality through our thinking. Accidents will happen. An act of aggression will spark a war that pulls in the whole world. In our personal lives, too, all kinds of things will come out of the blue— meetings and partings, love and betrayal.

It struck me as very strange that I could know this and forget this, slipping back into the trance of thinking mind, driven by the fear and unease those thoughts engendered. I didn't want to miss my life, spending my time on earth sleepwalking—well, sleep-running. The truth cannot be thought, a wise teacher once said to me. Sitting in my smashed up car, I realized what that meant. Even as tears flowed, I realized there is another way to live—I could see past this thinking mind and open to receiving the truth that is always being offered. I could start in that very moment.

"Don't turn away," counseled Rumi. "Keep your gaze on the bandaged place. That's where the light enters you."[10]

As an exercise, give yourself time every day to sit still and just do nothing. It can be five minutes to start. We practice opening to a new reality by being present with everything that is arising, including difficult feelings—little ripples of fear or embarrassment or molten thoughts and feelings that can't be named. Notice that life beyond— the quality of the light, the air that you breathe, the life around you. Notice that warmth of the life inside you. And notice that it is only the thinking mind that thinks it needs to be doing, commenting, reacting. If you wish, tell about what is present, allowing everything to be just like it is.

12

A Shared World

As he lay dying, the Buddha advised his beloved cousin and disciple Ananda to tell his followers to be islands unto themselves. I thought of this as I stood in a security line in the Indira Gandhi International Airport in New Delhi, just after a male security guard gestured for me to move to the line marked "Ladies."

I knew there were different translations that encouraged people to be "lamps" or "lights" unto themselves. Yet somehow I failed to notice there were separate security lines for "Ladies" and "Gents." I knew that both "island" and "lamp" were signified by the word *dīpa* in Pali, the language of the Buddhist scriptures, a Sanskrit-derived language that is probably close to what the Buddha spoke. But I didn't actually speak Pali—or Hindi or Gujarati, the Sanskrit-derived languages spoken in this airport and in the northern Indian city of Ahmedabad, where I was headed.

I was an American woman traveling alone, and it suddenly seemed clear that this was what I knew about India—bits of teachings of the Buddha, a bit of history about Gandhi, the storylines of a few novels and films. Some of this material was great, even sacred, but as I passed through a second round of security only to make the same mistake about "Ladies" and "Gents," it seemed to be nothing but a cloud of disembodied facts floating through my head like space junk.

The contrast between this kind of knowledge—a collection of facts, images, and dreams—and real *knowing*, real embodied awareness, felt crucial. I had read the invitation to the Gandhi 3.0 retreat in my living room north of New York City, while sitting in a pool of lamplight, watching snow fill up the pines outside my window. In that snowbound hush, in a house as cocooned from the outside world as a ship at night, I felt sure that I should go.

"You will not find these heroes on TV," the invitation read, referring to the sixty businesspeople, spiritual cultivators, social activists, and entrepreneurs who were to take part. "They don't seek glory, nor do they wear any uniforms. Sometimes they do normal jobs but they are often doing the real work in subtle and invisible ways."

I was being invited to be a secret agent of change by Nipun Mehta, founder of a community called ServiceSpace and leader of a gentle revolution of values called the Gift Economy or "giftivism." The Indian group hosting the retreat was Moved By Love, connected to Mehta and the California-based ServiceSpace the way aspen trees can be outcroppings of the same interconnected root system.

I had dreamed of being in India since I was a little girl. I remembered climbing over the furniture of our brick ranch house in northern New York, pretending I was padding through a jungle in India, my black panther consort by my side.

Were there black panthers in India? I had no idea. It was as if I had been practicing tracking something—practicing going toward something important. In the hugely self-centered, elaborately daydreamy yet completely innocent way that children have, I had sensed that I could be part of a greater life, one that involved my whole body and not just my head in school. I had sensed that my small life might be capable of a nobility my parents didn't suspect.

I typed "yes" to the invitation to the retreat almost as soon as I received it. Its phrasing touched my childhood sense that there was another way to live.

Yet now here I was in the real India, exposed. Faced with the unknown, it seemed clear that my mind's strong tendency was to seek the known, to plan and picture and think about familiar things rather than to engage in fresh seeing and experiencing. My wish to be here and to experience another, larger way to be in this world was real. But it seemed such a small soft light inside, like a night light, easy to miss in the glare. It was real, just much weaker than the habit of fear.

Outside the airport in Ahmedabad, Neerad, a volunteer from the retreat, held up a sign with my name on it. He took my bag and ushered me to a car with a quiet dignity that contrasted with a sign that read "We Love You." As we made our way through the streets of the city—through the indescribable inrush of Indian traffic and colors and contrasts and cows—I realized how tense I had been, checking and rechecking for my passport and the letter with the contact information.

At every turn on this trip so far, people had warned me to be careful, to be safe. In the car it dawned on me that help also kept appearing. "Just so you know," said an Indian woman waiting to board the plane at JFK, "Indian people don't have the same need for personal space. There will be crowding." The young Indian woman sitting next to me offered travel tips. In New Delhi, another Indian woman bought me a bottle of water and offered me a mobile phone to call home—and her phone number just in case. I came to India braced for darkness. But in all my planning, I hadn't anticipated the light. It dawned on me that those women and Neerad were islands, not self-sufficient as my conditioning led me to be, but refuges offering a bit of shelter.

We drove up a long road to the retreat center that is part of the Environmental Sanitation Institute. This creation by Ishwar Patel, a beloved man who dedicated his life to bringing sanitation and dignity to the people of India—especially women—is an oasis, a beautiful gated compound with gardens and a pond ringed by palm trees.

A posse of smiling people holding smiley-face signs, including Nipun Mehta, met me at the gate. I was surrounded, hugged, sung to. Weeks later, I was told that the group conferred about my reaction. They thought I had looked so shocked that they decided to tone their welcome down in the future. I was embarrassed to hear this, but that greeting was quite a blast of light and warmth to encounter in the dark of night.

After accepting the invitation to the retreat, I had received the beguiling response, "Great! We'll be here to welcome you home." Over the next few weeks, I learned that this practice of *welcoming home* (as if they knew about my childhood jungle-girl fantasy games), this giving without restraint or expectation of return, was an aim of the retreat and of Moved By Love. The greeting party at the gate was made up of volunteers from all over India and California, people who had come to practice service, to weave a net of *maitrī* or lovingkindness, to carry the spirit of Mahatma Gandhi into a new age.

I was given dinner and shown to a dorm-like compound and a room that featured narrow little beds with handsewn coverings and a single blanket. There were slatted wooden blinds without glass in the windows, a simple bathroom with a bucket and pitcher for a shower. The austerity created a feeling of elegant simplicity, peace, order, of living without wasting, of being mindful of the many without clean water.

Like everything else in the retreat center, my room was simple but beautiful, showing signs of great care, immediately exposing my sprawling American style, suitcase top flipped open, possessions taken out and arranged rather than folded and stowed, taking up space.

Told I would be solo for a few nights, I felt a wave of relief. I wanted to bolt the door, to be alone, to think about all I had been through—all of this in such stark contrast to the river of hospitality I was carried in on, to the little handmade gifts and offerings on the bed and tables, to the paper flower saying "Be the Change" on the mirror in the bathroom. It was never so clear how much of my life, including my spiritual life, involved isolation—stepping out, yes, but always retreating, seeking privacy and locked doors.

I went to sleep to sounds of music from a riotous Indian wedding blasting over scratchy speakers in a park somewhere and awoke to the sound of chanted prayers and bells and dogs barking and the smell of spice and woodsmoke along with strange new bird cries and new light.

From the depths of my body, a barely verbal insight dawned that I had come all this way because we are meant to live in our bodies, not just in our minds. We are meant to give ourselves to life, to take in impressions and receive energies too fine for words. Briefly, it was clear that a single choice exists, moment after moment. We can turn away from life or be open to receive. I vowed to try to be open.

Yet after my first bucket shower and a strong cup of chai, my head was back to wondering what the heart and aim of this big diffuse movement or organization really were. In the dining hall at breakfast, I confessed this to Guri Mehta, the wife of Nipun, who suggested I try just feeling with my heart instead of thinking. Guri said this with a California warmth and friendly intimacy that made me trust what she offered.

After Guri left, I was invited to sit at a table with a smiling man dressed in immaculate white. I was told he had been born and raised on the Gandhi Ashram. From his equanimity and quiet presence, I assumed he was a kind of monk, a modern *satyagrahi*, a renunciate love warrior, dedicated to truth. Deep in conversation with a group of young men who listened to him closely, like acolytes, he looked at me kindly and said in Hindi (which was translated for me), "Only things that can open can blossom." I knew this was a conclusion to a long exchange, but it felt uncanny, as if he knew about my waking insight and fleeting vow about opening.

Later I would learn that he was Jayesh Patel, the son of Ishwar Patel, the founder of the Sanitation Institute and the retreat center, and my host. In the coming weeks, I learned that Jayeshbhai (*bhai* means "brother" in Hindi and Gujarati, the local language of the district of Gujarat) is incredibly engaged. The founder of Manav Sadhna, an organization that works with ten thousand children, he is the managing trustee of the Sabarmati Ashram and the president of the Gujarat Harijan Sevak Sangh, a vast organization founded by Gandhi.

But I experienced him the way a child might, just noticing that his eyes were kind and didn't look away. He gave his attention in a way that few people ever do, without distraction or calculation. It was a warm embrace of a gaze, a granting of unconditional acceptance. Strangest and rarest of all was the feeling that all of this giving was effortless, that we were all on the same level and this love was like sunlight, as much mine as his.

"When we see our role in society as servants, we will light up the sky together like countless stars on a dark night," read a young woman named Kushmita in the opening circle, quoting Vinoba Bhave, a scholar and close spiritual friend of Gandhi, little known today in the West but revered in India, especially in this gathering: "Don't think of society as the sky on a full moon night. The moon's harsh light blinds us to the true and humble work of the stars. But on a moonless night, the true servants shine forth, as though they are connected invisibly in this vast and infinite cosmos."[11]

The intention of the retreat was to explore modern manifestations of Gandhi's values. Rooted in the principle that real change must start with inner transformation and we must be the change we wish to see in the world, it sought to shift away from a focus on great leaders and toward acts of "many-to-many," small acts of kindness, relationships not results. Slowly and carefully, they intended to weave a net of maitrī.

Lacking Hindi or much else in the way of real knowledge, I had no choice but to keep on observing and living like a child: being cared for, helpless to do much more than be present in the body in the most basic way. At every turn, I was met by small acts of kindness and generosity. I hadn't brought a towel; a folded towel appeared on the end of my bed. I lamented that I didn't have the right clothes, only purple sneakers and Western items; sandals showed up and a loose, cotton shirt or kurta.

Much that was valuable was in what was said and done during the retreat, but for me it was a teaching in surrender, in receiving gifts as they came and life as it came. In conditions that gave me almost no control and no opportunity to give back, I had no choice but to receive and to understand that receiving is not separate from giving.

On the anniversary of Gandhi's death, the whole retreat transferred to his Sabarmati Ashram in the suburbs of Ahmedabad. From this austere place, Gandhi led the Salt March and the Independence Movement. I sat in Gandhi's room, not normally open to the public, surrounded by his few possessions, his desk, walking stick, the iconic spinning wheel (or *charkha*), marveling at what had been accomplished here.

Days later, some of us returned to the ashram for morning prayers, then went out into the slums to visit schools and a women's center to see how Gandhi's work is being carried on today. Through it all, I watched Jayeshbhai. Often, he moved slowly or sat still, seeming to be empty of agenda or obvious care, yet meeting an endless stream of people, greeting everyone from slum kids to business leaders with the unwavering warmth and attention I experienced on that first day. I began to understand what the Buddha meant by being an island. He meant to land, to come down out of the head and enter the body and the present moment, to be in a peaceful, grounded state, nongrasping and nonafraid.

Jayeshbhai reminded me through a translator that Gandhi took his inspiration from the people in the villages he served. One day, a few of us were taken to visit a village where people live as most people have always lived, cooking over fires, working very hard for food and water, dependent on the help of oxen and camels and other animals, relying on the help of God and of each other. I rode on an oxcart and had tea with a saintly village elder.

After many hours I began to feel weak from the heat and hunger and also from an uneasy sense of being a tourist, as if my Western thought-filled self were trapping me outside the experience, as if my mind were a pesky fly buzzing behind glass. Just then, a woman waved us over, inviting us to sit down and share the bread she was baking over a fire. It was a slow gesture, in the natural order of things, and it reached through the glass.

Give us this day our daily bread. I wondered why it had never dawned on me before that this seemingly ordinary thing, this basic experience of the body, was also an act of faith. It struck me that the people I met in India, Ivy League–educated volunteers and Fulbright scholars and villagers alike, lived as if God were watching, as if everything mattered, and as if their smallest actions were a way of expressing their faith in this truth.

It touched me to remember that this understanding is in the Western tradition also. In *The Complete Mystical Works of Meister Eckhart*, it is explained that one of the last things the great German mystic said to his students was: "I will give you a rule, which is the keystone of all that I have ever said, which comprises all truth that can be spoken of or lived. It often happens that what seems trivial to us is greater in God's sight than what looms large in our eyes. Therefore we should accept all things equally from God, not ever looking and wondering which is greater, or higher, or better."[11]

In the days to come, I traveled more, flying to the heart of India to stay briefly at an ashram established by Vinoba in Maharashtra for the spiritual development of women, rare in India, and also at Gandhi's Sevagram Ashram. I kept on traveling as a child would, clueless about where I was going, handed a ticket to the "Spice Jet" to Nagpur, driven in a car arranged by Jayeshbhai, stopping to walk out into a field of organic cotton to watch the sunset, then stopping again for chai and to visit one of the countless temples we passed in the dark.

Along the way, Nipun told me that a Buddhist monk he knows said that probably every inch of India has witnessed a prayer or a bow. Before the New York editor in me could say that I doubted every inch, I realized that in my case this was literally true. Every inch of my trip, I had been carried on a kind of collective prayer, a collective intention to manifest maitrī.

At the Vinoba Ashram, we joined nuns for evening prayers among relics fifteen hundred years old. Conditions were very austere—my bed was basically a board. Yet there was a feeling of extraordinary safety. As elsewhere, there was very little privacy or private property, but people were eager to share food and prayer and stories.

Everyone was expected to share in the work. In predawn darkness, I slowly chopped vegetables. After the sun rose, I helped harvest turmeric. I was handed big roots to break apart, the easy work, just so I could play a part. At times, I felt as if a door in my heart were beginning to open. I saw that what mattered wasn't my rather shaky outer performance. The crucial point was opening to receive life and learning to become a vehicle for an energy or light of truth, just as I was.

As we dug turmeric, a nun with an incredible face approached. It was the kind of face that makes you not fear getting old—a safe face, not wanting, not hiding. She told us that she was eighty-five years old. We learned that she had spent twelve years on a walking pilgrimage across India, inspired by her teacher Vinoba who had walked the length and breadth of India over twenty years and persuaded wealthy landlords to give their landless neighbors a portion of their land. Ultimately more than four million acres were donated, one conversation at a time. The nun told us that while her body wasn't as strong now, she received energy from us.

The next day, we visited Gandhi's Sevagram Ashram. Gandhi deliberately founded this "village for service" in the heart of India even though it was (and is) very out of the way. After the Salt March, he vowed not to return to Ahmedabad and not to leave the heart of the country until independence was achieved. The atmosphere in Sevagram was quiet and reverent. Signs ask for "Silence." It was clear that something great happened here.

It also felt strangely modern. Electricity was generated by biofuel from the cows, the dishwater funneled into the compost that helped grow the organic vegetables we ate for lunch. Sitting on the ground where Gandhi had sat to think and write and serve, physically in touch with the radical simplicity of the conditions of his life, it was easy to see that he was a visionary. Once *swaraj* or self-rule for India was attained, he knew it was important to continue to evolve. He often said, "my quest continues," that the goal was "*sarvodaya*: the advancement of all." Gandhi knew there can be no peace unless we learn to live in a shared world.

After we left Sevagram, four of us headed to the airport in Nagpur: Nipun; Nimesh (or Nimo) Patel, a former rap star and Wharton School graduate who has created a service-based music venture called Empty Hands Music; Anne Veh, an artist and curator from California; and myself—all but Anne bound for Mumbai. We hit a massive traffic jam. After nearly an hour, we decided to walk it. "Prepare to be stared at," said Nipun.

Off we went, two American women and two Indian men trudging down a highway against traffic, carrying luggage. Soon, a police officer stopped us and asked us what we thought we were doing, contributing a drop more disorder to this hopeless-seeming mess. Nipun explained with a smile that we were late for our flight. He spoke in Hindi so I didn't understand what was being said, but I saw that he spoke in such a way that the officer started flagging down vehicles to find us a ride. A bus full of civil servants in uniform stopped and opened their doors, even insisting that Anne and I put down our bags and take seats up front.

As it unfolded, it felt like being in an Indian version of *Alice in Wonderland.* But as I sat smiling at a bus full of smiling people in uniform, all of them enjoying this unexpected adventure in generosity that started by stopping and opening their doors to the unexpected, it struck me that I hadn't fallen down a rabbit hole so much as fallen into life, into the dense, complex, inrushing life of India, life as it can feel without fear.

Nipun means "master." Watching the scene unfold in the traffic jam, I glimpsed a new (although I knew it was also ancient) kind of life mastery, a way of being unguarded and on intimate terms with life. I didn't think this realization so much as feel the living, embodied truth behind things I had read and heard. I once heard Mozart's music described as innocent, heedless of the world and heedless of shame. I thought of the Buddha walking through India, teaching people to be islands in the stream of life, abiding peacefully and mindfully. I thought of Jayeshbhai, quoting his father Ishwar Patel, telling him to "Create heaven wherever you are."

As I left to fly home to New York, Jayeshbhai, Nipun, Guri, and others came out to the gates of the retreat center to hug me goodbye. Jayeshbhai presented me with a beautiful scarf woven from organic cotton by women in the slum. "Tell them we are meant to live in a shared world," he said.

The journey begins with a willingness just to stop and notice what is happening right now. Just that. Just notice with an attitude of kind willingness to receive whatever comes.

Most of us yearn to be more present in our lives, equating presence with a greater sense of wholeness and ease in the world. Yet, when we turn our attention to what is happening right now, we most often feel dissatisfied, as if elements are missing or off. It's too hot or too cold, or it may be a beautiful day but we are stuck inside or in traffic or have too much to do. We say no to what is happening and imagine some future better moment when we will be able to yes. Someday, we tell ourselves, we will be able to be fully present. When things are better, we will be able to have serene equanimity with what is happening. We don't realize that this attitude of no doesn't lead to yes.

Generosity begins with being generous toward ourselves, letting everything be just as it is. This attitude of acceptance does not mean compliance with bad treatment or bad conditions. Just the opposite. It means being willing to open to what is happening, allowing reality to appear.

A Buddhist monk I know once embarked on the experiment of walking the length of New York City, holding his begging bowl—not asking for anything, just holding it, walking serenely along, open to what came.

"What did I get?" he asked, pausing to let his gaze wander around the room in the upstate New York monastery where a small group of his Western students sat, a look of triumphant glee on his face. "I received the great gift of emptiness."

Emptiness—the Buddha's great insight into the nature of life. Everything is connected to everything else. This insight frees us from a sense of separation from life. It also frees us from clinging. We, too, are part of nature. I thought this was a great takeaway from the experiment, a much better gift than the gum wrappers and paper cups or even the loose bills and spare change that might have come. This particular monk, a brilliant translator of the early Buddhist teachings, is Brooklyn-born and raised, so the empty bowl or even, potentially, the trash couldn't have come as a surprise.

Under the punch line, there was a deeper observation: New York City, and this culture as a whole, was not used to seeing monastics going on alms rounds. We aren't used to people who aren't selling or hustling but just open to receive what is freely given.

For a short time, try practicing this way. Allow yourself to be with what is happening at any given moment, adding nothing, rejecting nothing, just being open to reality as it is. This practice can be especially nourishing and helpful at those times when you feel tired or ill or when conditions make life seem too difficult or desolate. Bring your attention down out of your weary mind into the body. Allow yourself to exhale completely, as if it's your last breath. Don't push. Just let it go. Notice how the next breath fills your lungs naturally. Notice how life comes to you. Let go of all striving and notice the current of life and presence that is inside you and outside you. Notice that you are part of a greater whole.

13

Saturday in New York with Gitanjali

Gitanjali Babbar wanted to walk to the Freedom Tower. This cold day in New York City marked the end of her first trip to the United States. She had visited Washington, D.C.; Reno, Nevada; the Bay Area; and now for a few days, New York. For six weeks, Gitanjali had been a U.S. Department of State Professional Fellow, broadening her already deep knowledge of sex trafficking by observing how it manifests in this country. The night before she had visited a Manhattan strip club, hoping to talk with or at least observe the interactions of the women who worked there.

The workers in the strip club seemed lonely and competitive compared to women in the Indian brothels, she told me as we walked south. One young woman in particular haunted her because she wasn't as attractive as the other workers and seemed intent on using her earnings on plastic surgery, desperate to be a more appealing object.

My plan was Central Park, the Metropolitan Museum of Art, lunch, and tea—a day apart from all places associated with great suffering. Yet Gitanjali didn't want to separate from the suffering of others. She walked toward it smiling.

Gitanjali said she loved the way people walk in New York, striding along fast and free, "everyone walking everywhere." Bundled in a dark wool coat, eyes bright with excitement, interested in everything, the twenty-seven-year-old looked younger than she does in pictures and video clips, more like a visiting college student than a visionary and activist. In Delhi she doesn't have the chance to walk like this, she said. On G.B. Road in Delhi, where the brothels are, nobody goes walking. Most never leave their buildings, and some of the youngest can't leave their cells. Before Gitanjali, no young woman would set one foot there by choice.

By day, G.B. (for Garstin Bastion) Road is a hardware district, full of auto repair garages and shops selling engine parts. At night, the shutters come down and the sex trade takes over. The second and third floors of the buildings on G.B. Road house seventy-seven brothels or *kothas*, four thousand women and fifteen hundred children, making it the largest and most notorious red-light district in Delhi. On the second floor of one of these brothels, Gitanjali founded Kat-Katha, a refuge and resource for these women and children who have become like family to her.

"I don't feel safe in Delhi," she told me. "But I feel safe on G.B. Road."

Gitanjali's mother wanted her to be a teacher. "She thought that was a proper job for a girl," a noble profession that was also safe and contained, "at work by seven and home again after two." But Gitanjali didn't want to live in a safe container. Longing to go out and explore worlds she didn't know, she became a journalist only to discover that editors treat the world like a market, assigning pieces based on what they think will sell. "I didn't want to live in a market," she explained, so she entered a world sustained by different laws.

Gitanjali joined the Gandhi Fellowship and lived for two years in the rural village of Rajasthan, India. The Gandhi Fellowship is a two-year intensive program that immerses batches of talented young Indians in real social problems, sending them into rural villages and government schools, aiming to cultivate inner and outer transformation—transfiguring the quality of education while cultivating leadership skills informed by Gandhian values.

"When my parents dropped me off, they stayed nearby in a guesthouse, hoping I would drive home with them." Gitanjali visited them once for a shower, but then she went back to the village and stuck it out. Over time, the girl who didn't want to be a teacher learned to improve rural education by engaging kids and teachers and parents, fostering cooperation, activating change by seeing that in every situation there are multiple perspectives and stakeholders. Her time in the Gandhi Fellowship planted the seeds she needed to found Kat-Katha.

Yet Kat-Katha wasn't really *founded*, Gitanjali explained; it evolved. After the fellowship, Gitanjali worked for a health organization that sent her into the brothels to interview the sex workers about contraceptives and other health topics. Yet that way of questioning, as if there were a wall between herself and these women, made her uncomfortable. Something about these women touched her. She began visiting the brothels after work, talking with the women and learning how they came to be on G.B. Road.

And then came a turning point. One afternoon, when she came to interview women, she found a circle of women prepared to ask *her* questions about her own life. Where did she live? Did she have a boyfriend? She didn't know what to say. Gitanjali quit her job and began spending whole days at the brothel getting to know the women more deeply, gaining their trust. One day an older woman asked her to teach her something. And Gitanjali, who had never set out to be a teacher, began bringing books. Other women noticed and joined in, and soon their children came.

At home at night, she shared her experiences on social media, and over time volunteers began to show up. Three years later, Kat-Katha has 120 volunteers and is working with the women of all seventy-seven brothels on G.B. Road. Gitanjali speaks of all this matter-of-factly, marveling at the serendipity of events. Someone donated bookbinding machines. A business donated used paper. And they began to teach the women how to bind and craft notebooks. The children began to see themselves as artists and revealed an uncanny ability to attract the help they needed. A student wanted to learn to dance, and a volunteer appeared to teach her.

"We call Kat-Katha magic, but it's not magic," Gitanjali told me as the Freedom Tower came into view. "What is happening is the answer to the prayers of these women and children."

"I never would have dreamed we would have volunteers from Google come visit," adds Gitanjali, who had gone to the Google offices in New York the day before. She described a group of young American women coming to Kat-Katha with huge bodyguards in tow. The women insisted the bodyguards stay downstairs when they went up to the second floor. When they came downstairs, the bodyguards asked if they could go upstairs themselves.

Recently, the Gandhi Ashram in Delhi offered Gitanjali an unused ashram building to serve as a hostel for the children of the brothel, an act of grace that will pull the girls away from the almost certain risk of being sold into prostitution, the boys away from a world saturated in drugs and alcohol and the sex trade. There the children will be taught reading and crucial academic skills but also basic human skills of washing, brushing teeth, being kind. The school is modeled on the school for children housed within the famous Gandhi Ashram at Sabarmati in Ahmedabad, which was the starting point of Gandhi's Salt March, the home of the Indian Independence Movement.

To Gitanjali, Kat-Katha is an alternative space full of passionate volunteers who lead by example. Within this space she sees amazing exchanges happen, which she describes in simple terms: people meet and share stories and love. Yet what Gitanjali and Kat-Katha do is courageous and visionary, a practice in selfless service. Kat-Katha is skillfully bringing about radical change, quietly replacing the usual commerce of the brothel with community, caring, hope.

Gitanjali and her fellow volunteers take inspiration, as do many other "servant leaders," from Vinoba Bhave (1895–1982), a scholar, activist, and trusted spiritual friend and adviser of Gandhi. Called Acharya ("teacher" in Sanskrit), Vinoba cared deeply about creating a just and equitable society, about helping good triumph over evil, generosity over greed. A frail man, he walked all over India, asking the rich to donate land he then gave to the landless poor.

Vinoba taught a new movement of social transformation, not dependent on a charismatic leader but focusing instead on the power of connection, with many small groups making many efforts, many connecting to many, creating a network for the good. He is the one who said, as Kushmita shared on our retreat in India: "When we see our role in society as servants, we will light up the sky together like countless stars on a dark night. . . . The moon's harsh light blinds us to the true and humble work of the stars. But on a moonless night, the true servants shine forth, as though they are connected invisibly in this vast and infinite cosmos."

At last, we saw the Freedom Tower looming up straight ahead. I told Gitanjali it was the tallest structure in New York, 1,776 feet tall in honor of our Declaration of Independence. She asked me what it was like being in New York on the day the World Trade Center was struck. I told her a few of the good things I remembered—the kindness and caring that spontaneously appeared, strangers talking to strangers, helping each other home.

"We were all so scared when it happened," she said simply. "We thought that if it happened here it could happen to us." And it did happen in India, in Mumbai in November 2008 when ten Pakastani men associated with the terror group Lashkar-e-Tayyiba launched a series of attacks over four days, killing 164 people. And so much else happened, and continues to happen.

We lingered for a long time at the National September 11 Memorial, watching the water spill down into the two huge fountain pools that fill the footprints of the Twin Towers. The pools themselves are dark and still and seemingly bottomless, so that it feels as if the water is spilling down into mystery. "Now they are all together," said Gitanjali, opening her fingers in a gesture of release. I thought of something I heard at the Gandhi Ashram about the potential of selfless service: "We go from emptiness to oneness."

Later, I discovered that the workers and volunteers at the memorial had launched an effort called "Tribute 2983," dedicating themselves and inviting others to perform 2,983 acts of generosity and kindness in honor of the victims of the attacks, by replacing violence with compassion, honoring lives lost by paying kindness forward. No wonder Gitanjali wanted to visit.

At last Gitanjali admitted to being a little hungry and cold and tired. I led her to lunch in an Indian restaurant I knew. She ordered vegetarian food for us to share, then she closed her eyes and prayed in silence before we ate. Over curry and naan, we talked more about the painful realities of life in the brothels. Gitanjali pointed to boxed air vents in the ceiling, barely big enough for a slender person to crawl through, indicating that this is about the size of the cells that abducted girls are kept in.

These ten-, eleven-, twelve-year-old girls are cocooned in such constricted cells for three to four years, never leaving, seeing only "special" customers ("special" in the sense that they pay extra and won't go to the police). The girls are confined like this until they are judged by brothel owners to be too broken and too afraid to run away. I asked her how this can happen. These girls are abducted from poor families, she explained. "The poor have no resources to find their children."

When the girls become women, they rarely leave the brothel. When a woman has a baby, the baby is often taken away from her.

She is allowed to see the child once a week as an inducement to stay. There is no medical care. Gitanjali described seeing a young woman with sores related to AIDS; the woman was untreated because the brothel owner thought that treatment would be bad for business. The usual diet is very poor, mostly only bread and street food. Given drink and drugs and the squalid lifestyle, the average life expectancy is about forty-five years old. The women who manage to grow that old are sent out to procure customers on G.B. Road.

As the painful details mounted, I wondered who frequents these brothels. Poor men? Rich men? Sometimes rich men come to G.B. Road, Gitanjali answered. There are special places where incredible services are offered. There are brothels featuring young Nepalese girls who are very beautiful and blue-eyed.

Gitanjali told me that one of her biggest challenges is to not judge, not even the brothel owners. "They come to me and say, 'Look at this expensive suit I'm wearing. But what good is it to be able to have money if my children can't get an education?'" Gitanjali plans to include their children, shamed and shunned because of what their fathers do, in the new hostel school. All must be included.

Offering me the bowl of rice, Gitanjali reminded me that Jayesh Patel, a beloved mentor and leader in the Gandhi organization, believes that it's a sin to waste food. Suddenly, the big basket of naan and big platter of rice seemed a display of abundance for display's sake, and this waste obscurely connected to the exploitation and neglect of these girls and women. As Gitanjali offered me yet more bread and more rice, it struck me that the seeming magic of Kat-Katha, like all magic, involves seeing what is usually unseen.

Kat-Katha means "puppet show." Gitanjali told me that the name came from an insight she had had from spending time with the women in the brothel, learning about their lives and how they wound up on G.B. Road—one kidnapped as a child, one lured by a false promise of marriage, most born into grinding poverty. She saw that we each are the product of a long chain of cause and effect, all controlled by the strings of our circumstances and conditioning. She saw that the difference between her and the women in the brothel was that her strings "were in better hands."

We walked north, to Central Park and the Metropolitan Museum. At the Conservatory Water in the park, we stopped and watched the radio-controlled model sailboats gliding slowly on still water, their white sails as touching as the wings of great birds. Gitanjali exclaimed at the storybook beauty of the scene, asking me to take her picture at the Alice in Wonderland statue. "I'm going to read *Alice in Wonderland* to my kids and then show the picture to them." She missed her family—her parents with whom she lives in Delhi, her boyfriend, and her family on G.B. Road.

"While I am here roaming through New York, there are 120 people working hard," she said. She doesn't want to be the head of an organization or a movement, she told me. She was reassured when Jayesh Patel told her that in time the movement itself would take over and she would sink into the background. It struck me as strange that we usually think of heroes as solitary, standing strong and alone, protected by the armor of their convictions. It struck me that I was spending the day with someone whose idea of heroism consisted in taking off her armor, in making herself vulnerable to life, giving up the privilege of separation.

At the Metropolitan Museum of Art, we stood before a magnificent sculpture of the Hindu Trinity: Brahma, Vishnu, Shiva—the gods of creation, maintenance, and destruction. We ended with Ganesh, the god of beginnings, patron of wisdom and learning, overcomer of obstacles. Gitanjali told me that she has always loved Ganesh.

"I haven't yet met one American who wants war," said Gitanjali as we walked out into the twinkling New York night. I assured her they exist. "Those are the people I would like to talk with," she said.

We walked down Fifth Avenue to Grand Central Station, where Gitanjali was meeting the friend who would host her that night. The stores were being elaborately decorated for Christmas. Many had their windows shrouded in black to save the surprise until after Thanksgiving, the unofficial start of the Christmas holiday season.

As we passed the Christmas tree at Rockefeller Center, still under wraps before the official lighting, she told me someone had given her a bough from the tree. She had packed it in her suitcase. "I plan to tell my kids about Christmas and about New York, then I'm going to show it to them."

In Grand Central Station, she bought me a notebook decorated with a web of sparkles, "to write down what we talked about." As she left, I thought of Vinoba Bhave's vision of stars on a moonless night, of the infinite web of connection.

> The mind creates the abyss, the heart crosses it.
> —*SRI NISARGADATTA MAHARAJ*[12]

If we take stock of things with the mind alone, the odds can seem stacked against us. The devastation of the environment, poverty, human trafficking—it can all seem overwhelming. Where to start?

Recently, I took a walk on a bitter cold winter day. I stopped at a landing and looked out over a frozen lake. The scene was beautiful in a stark, primordial way—silver sky, silver lake. I imagined life during the Ice Age. But the dominant thought was: "Left to my own resources, I would die out here in a very short time."

And yet. Maybe I am not the heartiest in my tribe, and maybe I don't know how to start a fire without matches. But according to the Buddha, we are also endowed with qualities of heart that he called "divine" and "immeasurable." Usually, they are broken down into four: lovingkindness or friendliness; compassion; appreciative joy, which is the ability to delight in other beings' happiness and good fortune; and equanimity, which is the calm born of wisdom (including the wisdom that everything passes).

Would any or all of these qualities help me survive in a raw, cold landscape? There is some pretty good science that tells us that positive emotions can steady and broaden the mind, helping us see more and find creative solutions—where to take shelter, etc. But the heart also crosses the abyss by reminding us, not in words but in feelings, that we belong to life. This is not to say that life is always easy. But there is also kindness, compassion, joy, and possibility. Even on the coldest day.

The Buddhist word for the energy and effort necessary for awakening, *viriya*, comes from a Sanskrit word that meant "hero" or "strong and virile man." But in my experience, practicing in the thick of life, the energy that is required is subtler—and definitely not restricted to a specific gender. What is needed is more of an effort of the heart—a willingness to open to see and be with rather than an act of will. The hero's journey becomes an inner quest that begins with gentle questioning: *Can I be with this right now? Can I let go of my attachment to a belief or a story about the past and about who I am?* Notice how it feels to let yourself be with what is, just for a moment, resting in an awareness that is calm and compassionate and open.

14

You Would Run for Your Life

"You would run for your life," my daughter said. "You would grab a few precious things and run as fast as you could."

We were traveling by train along the English coast, bound for Edinburgh in Scotland. The sun was glinting on the North Sea, and we looked across it in the general direction of Denmark, the homeland of my mother's parents. My daughter, who was studying medieval history in graduate school, was describing what it would be like to live in an English coastal village in the Middle Ages and see Viking sails on the horizon.

She had grown up hearing that her American mother was a proud descendant of Vikings, and not just any old raiders, but nobles. How could we know this? And why take such pride? Maybe it was because we are American and have few reminders of Viking raids.

Although both her parents came from Denmark, my mother grew up on the Great Plains of western Nebraska. She inherited this story from her mother, who probably inherited it from hers, and so on. My heart twisted to remember how frail and sad my mother became in what I call her "reclining years" because she spent her days curled up in a big leather recliner by the window. Although she lived in Florida, it was as if a Nordic winter had come over her and never lifted.

Still, she smiled whenever the subject of Vikings came up. Yes, they were wild. Yes, they sacked monasteries. But they were family and lovable. This was the attitude. She saw their strengths as well as their weaknesses. They were brave and adventurous, and possibly they had seasonal affective disorder, like she and others in our family did. Think of how they suffered during those long dark winters.

As the train rolled along the coast, I told Alex that after my mother died I dreamed of a Viking funeral. I stood on a beach in Florida, watching a ship containing her body glide into the sunset. Certain metaphors seem built into these bodies and hearts, I told her, inherited from ancestors for whom the unknown really was beyond the horizon.

Our ancestors live on in us, in our DNA. This brain, heart, and body are structurally the same as those possessed by human beings 150,000 years ago. Our fundamental experience must be the same. Perhaps this deep commonality is why we sometimes feel the presence of loved ones.

My father had died a few months before and my daughter, who lives in England, arranged the trip as a way for us to be together and also as a pilgrimage. We were going to see Scotland, homeland of some of my father's ancestors, birthplace of his last name, and a place he had never been. We were going to stand on the land and look out at the hills and think about the lives they lived.

Alex loved her grandfather and lovingly planned this adventure as a balm for grief. But immediate family is one thing and ancestors another. She wondered why Americans seem to be so interested in discovering their ancestry—especially because my father's ancestors were among the earliest European settlers of New York, and I still was a New Yorker. Wasn't that place in particular the island of misfit toys, where people came to escape the limitations and expectations of their families and hometowns? Why look back?

We need roots and connection, I told her. For every American this is so, I thought—whether they came seeking freedom or in chains. People want to know where we came from, to be rooted in a deeper truth.

The sun sparkled on the North Sea. I was filled with a sense of the poignancy of life, the relentless way things and people are lost. I needed to say more. *Don't try to compare your life to the life of a younger person*, I thought to myself. This I knew. Even people who really love each other can't really understand what another experiences. But we still shouldn't hesitate to share our own deepest experience. As we age, we have quite a lot of it.

As the train left the coast and headed north, I told Alex about a dream that was more than an ordinary dream. It had happened years before, at a retreat center in California. The evening of the dream, a heated argument broke out in a big meditation hall about injustice. Disheartened, I left and went to bed, wondering how the wounds in this country could ever heal.

I woke up in another body, in another time and another place. I stood on the bow of a longship approaching a foreign shore. My body was different, bigger and stronger. But I was in that body, sensing the cold salt air on my skin and watching dawn wash the sky with color and light. The ship cut swiftly through the water. As we drew close to shore, I could see people standing and waiting amid dark trees.

My heart glowed like an ember, commanding my attention. This time would be different. I would take off the armor and put down the sword. I would open to receive what came instead of rushing in to take. The people on the shore stood watching, as tall and rooted as the trees. They were not running. I felt the others behind me in the ship, alert. It was a seemingly small act, opening a heart. But it was a momentous change.

The train crossed the border into Scotland. Alex looked like she didn't know what to say. I pressed on. After this dream, I had realized that I could make amends in this life. I could learn to take off my armor to open my heart and mind. This body, this heart, this brain, come to us from the ancestors. In a very real sense, they live in us.

We don't see this because we believe that time is linear, endless forward progress instead of cycles within cycles, day and night, seasons, heartbeats, breaths. Zen master Dogen said that when we sit down to practice, we sit down with the ancient ones, with the Buddha and all those who sought to wake up. They help us, and we help them. The First Australians call modern people the "line people" because we believe time is linear. If we woke up from this trance, we would understand that time doesn't exist in the way we think it does. We would understand that it is simply our turn to try. If this is true, we can repair the past and prepare a new future. In this very moment, in this body, with this heart.

"Think of it this way," I said to my daughter. "Have you had moments that seem to contain your whole life, moments in which everything you have been through seems to have been a preparation?" Alex nodded, smiling, possibly thinking of love.

"Maybe there are moments when others are present."

"Possible," said Alex, looking doubtful. The train rolled deeper into Scotland. "Actually, you're a mix of oppressor and oppressed," said Alex.

"Aren't we all?" I asked. Still, I knew what she meant. According to Ancestry.com my DNA is 41 percent Scandinavian, 39 percent British, 14 percent Irish, 4 percent Western European, 1 percent European Jewish, with a thrilling dash of Western Asia. My British-Irish blend paternal DNA was shared by people who were probably terrorized by the Vikings.

My 100 percent Danish mother possessed 9 percent non-Danish DNA, possibly related to some long-ago raid on a coastal village, but maybe due to someone falling happily in love and assimilating. And certainly there were people who shared my British and European and drop of West Asian DNA who oppressed others. *Everyone is mixed*, I thought.

The burning question is: How do we connect with our deeper humanity? How do we grow down and take root so that we can experience ourselves as part of a greater cycle, a member of a bigger family, not just someone carried along passively on a stream of change?

It doesn't matter where we start, I learned. It only matters that we let the questions deepen. We can start with notions so literal and weak they make us wince to think of later. I once visited an outdoor event in Lower Manhattan, for example, thinking this might help me enter into the experience of an early settler.

I had taken the Metro-North train down to Bowling Green Park to walk through what the *New York Times* said would be a colonial village set up to celebrate the four-hundredth anniversary of Henry Hudson's exploration of what would become the greater New York metropolitan area. Even though I knew there would be cheeses and little wooden shoes involved, I still thought I would be able to walk through humble little cottages that might remind me of what it was like to be here long ago. Instead, there were rows of little kiosks selling French fries, gouda, herring burgers, tulips, and, yes, little wooden shoes.

My father had roared with good-natured laughter when I told him about the New Amsterdam adventure, reminding me that our ancestors didn't stay long in Manhattan anyway. They migrated up the Hudson Valley to the banks of the St. Lawrence River and Lake Ontario, tilling rocky little farms or becoming sailing captains on the St. Lawrence River.

Because my mother was from the Great Plains, her story of our noble Viking ancestors flowed in with images I had of the Plains Indians. I pictured the Vikings crossing the great water in open boats, living close to nature, honoring gods who represented great forces. Like the Blackfoot, Cheyenne, and Lakota tribes, they were warriors who lived in the natural world in relationship with powerful forces. As a child, I made no distinction between continents. The big difference was between those whose lives included the body and nature and those who left it behind.

In a sense, discovering our genetic roots is like those marvelous stories about traveling the world only to find the treasure buried in your own backyard or in a chest under your own bed. And the ultimate trip came for me when I sent a scraping of cells from inside my cheek to the National Geographic's Genographic Project, a genetic population study that is attempting to track the migrations of our earliest common humanity based on the notches that get carved into our DNA as it is copied and passed down through the generations.

Months later, I received a world map that traced my matrilineal DNA back 150,000 years, to a woman in East Africa—our common genetic "Eve." We are all family.

But it was equally astonishing to discover that my mother's line belongs to "haplogroup X," a group whose DNA possesses markers in common with Lakota, Sioux, Ojibwa, Navajo, and other Indigenous Americans. I pictured Plains Indians carrying long boats to the Great Lakes, sailing up the St. Lawrence and across the open sea, to Denmark, where they taught the prehistoric Viking warriors how to build longships and sail across the open sea. The man I was in the vision and the people on shore were ultimately family. Everyone is related.

During his final journey, the Buddha gave the advice to his beloved disciple Ananda to "be islands unto yourselves, refuges unto yourselves. . . ." Facing death reveals the true nature of life: It passes. At times, it can feel as if we are being swept along.

When the Buddha spoke of being an island he didn't mean be cut off from the flow of life. By being an island, he meant dare to touch the earth of your own living experience in the present moment. He meant dare to relax and travel from the surface to the depths, from thinking and emotional reactions to deeper human feelings and insights. He meant to sit down and join the circle. He knew that when we return to the life of the body, the basic experience of being here—breathing in and out, sensing the air on the skin and the beating heart—can often blossom into a feeling of how good it is to be here. He knew that the simple act of returning to the breath and the body can return us to the great cycle of nature and to the ancestors. It can remind us how amazing it is to be alive. We may have a feeling of basic communion with others who live.

I thought of my father at the end of his life. Blind from macular degeneration and tethered to oxygen, he talked about basic experiences of life, about spending summers on a farm and how happy commanding officers were during World War II when they found they had farm boys among their soldiers "because they know how to do things." At the end of his life, my father knew what really matters. "Just sit with me, honey," he would say.

My father understood that no matter what is happening, we could sit down and be islands. Even with time rushing on, we can return to the basic experience of breathing in and out, hearts beating, being alive in the present moment.

"Isn't life a ball?" he used to ask when confronted with some fresh evidence of absurdity. Even when things grew tough, he rolled with it. "I know I can't go on forever, but I would like to keep going as long as I can, just to see how things unfold."

When we really understand that there is no escape from time's passage, no escape from life, we may find ourselves bringing our whole lives to each moment. Sometimes, we may even feel as if our ancestors are with us, witnessing life through our eyes. We may see that this awareness itself is a gift and that we can give back. We can find freedom for ourselves and those who came before.

On the last day of our stay in Edinburgh, Alex and I climbed to the top of Arthur's Seat, the main peak in a group of hills around Edinburgh, so named because it is claimed to be the location of King Arthur's Round Table. "Do you feel anything?" Alex asked as we climbed. I told her I did, but it wasn't what she thought. My father was gone. My mother was gone. My daughter was grown up and had moved to England. I thought of all of our ancestors back and back and back, of all that came before, that we should be here.

At the summit Alex and I listened to the wind and voices of the climbers around us. All humans carry the DNA of ancestors who traveled a long way, who were pushed from their lands by famine or earthquake or war or a deeper yearning.

In a famous letter, Albert Einstein offered guidance to an ordained rabbi who wrote explaining that he had tried in vain to comfort his 19-year-old daughter over the death of her 16-year-old sister: "A human being is a part of the whole, called by us 'Universe,' He experiences himself, his thoughts and feelings as something separated from the rest—a kind of optical delusion of his consciousness. The striving to free oneself from this delusion is one issue of true religion."[13]

I told Alex that my second cousin, who knows much about our family history, came to visit once and revealed that an ancestor in my mother's family possessed a large estate in Denmark in the twelfth century. I asked him how this could be known, and he said there were deeds of land going back to the fifteenth century. Before that there were legends.

"He probably was a Viking," said Alex. "In that period in Denmark, that was how a large estate was created."

That very ancestor could have stood on the bow of a longship. So could have the ancestors of my father. In a tourist shop in Edinburgh, we bought a pamphlet with a little plaid cover dedicated to the Cochrane clan (somewhere along our line the final e was dropped). Early on, the Cochrane clan was taken over by a Norseman. I had Vikings on both sides, as well as those they oppressed.

This probably wasn't really the place of Arthur's Round Table, Alex explained. And if any truth remained to the legend of Arthur, he wasn't a knight in shining armor or a king in a grand castle, but an earlier kind of warrior chief, living a life that was much simpler and more elemental. I sat and listened quietly, open to the wind and the possibilities.

In the middle of the day on a Tuesday just after Thanksgiving, on Park Avenue in Manhattan, I was assaulted and robbed. Of all places. As if any place is right. But still, it wasn't a dark and deserted side street. It was lunchtime on a crowded avenue.

I was meeting a friend from my meditation sangha for lunch. He was shaken by the death of a friend, and I wanted to sit with him and hear about her. But the subway from Brooklyn was delayed.

"Life," I texted my friend, after he texted saying that the subway he was on was just sitting in a tunnel. I meant that things never go exactly as planned. "Meditate," I texted, meaning just sit there and notice what is really happening. "Yes," he texted. "Thank you."

I thought I had found just the place for lunch. The café in Scandinavia House is quiet and cozy, decorated with twinkling lights, nestled behind a shop that is full of Scandinavian sweaters and scarves and little carved reindeer. A refuge.

"I'm out of Grand Central Station, on Park," he texted. "I will walk up and meet you," I answered. I was in the middle of texting "west side," meaning that the café and I were on the west side of Park Avenue, when I was tackled to the ground and relieved of my purse.

I saw and heard my assailant briefly before it happened: big, rough, American, no accent, straight dark hair, dark complexion. He rushed toward me, too close, muttering "donations, at least $5." Instinct made me veer away and step it up, leaving him behind me. But he must have turned and followed me. I was pushed hard and hit the sidewalk. I held on to the strap of my cross-body bag for dear life, but he pulled on it until the strap snapped. He was in a fury. I yelled for help, and three men took off. He knocked down one man who stepped in his path. A linebacker on meth. On something. And then he was gone.

My dear friend found me standing on a street corner talking to two English women who had witnessed the robbery. My thumb was bleeding from holding on and my knees were scraped and bloodied. Just like the men who instantly responded, running toward danger, he responded, holding my hand, applying Band-Aids and antiseptic and caring attention. This, too, is important to note.

I'm sharing this story because I am freshly reminded of certain crucial truths: All kinds of things happen to us in this world, including hard things. One way of understanding impermanence is that anything can happen at any time. We can be attacked, even sometimes by people who are supposed to be our protectors. We can be robbed, and maybe not just of our purses but of our trust and faith in love. And here comes the important truth: *It's Not Our Fault!*

There is a tendency in us to blame ourselves when bad things happen. This can be subtle—we split ourselves off from others or we split off that long-ago part that was abused or abandoned. We make it part of our story. *Did I attract this? Did I deserve this because I wasn't looking or leading him on? Am I cursed?* No!

In my case, I was wearing that little cross-body bag in front of my body because about seven years earlier my wallet had been stolen at JFK and I blamed myself—I wasn't paying attention; I was leaning over the luggage carousel; etc. And I've been robbed and mugged before.

Was I assaulted on Park Avenue because I looked weak? I've read that predators like to go after the cow that is apart from the herd, the spacey or sickly little cow. *Was that what I was to this man? Did I project some message that invited this?* No! I was a brave and upright dharma teacher, striding up Park Avenue to meet her friend. I was mindful and happily looking forward to seeing him. I was tackled from behind.

"It's true that you have suffered an unusual number of these incidents," said my sister. She happens to be the widow of a Navy pilot. "But then again, I know a young woman who was married to three pilots, and all of them died. She was widowed three times. Statistically improbable but true."

There is an even deeper truth. We have within us an enormous capacity to heal and open our lives. There is no time limit. The radical promise of the practice of presence is that we can *be* loving awareness. As we bring loving awareness to this body—extending gentle, patient compassionate attention to our feelings as they appear—we slowly settle down and open up like flowers.

"How are you feeling?" my friend asked.

"My body hurts. But mostly my feelings are really hurt. There is also sadness and fury."

He listened, putting little bits of hummus and pita bread on my plate, which I couldn't eat, pouring water. Sometimes—often—the best thing we can do for a friend is listen and offer glasses of water.

Life is unpredictable. Hard things happen to good people. The gift of presence is not the guarantee of safe passage, but the knowledge that what happens to us is not personal—not a commentary on our value. We are subject to forces large and small. I was in the path of my attacker—in the way of his aggression, his violent, probably trauma-driven need. Spiritual practice doesn't always prevent such things from happening any more than it can always prevent pain and heartache. Some very great teachers, including the Buddha, Jesus, and Moses, suffered injury, betrayal, or abandonment. But presence clears a way inside. It reminds us that we are more than what happened to us. It reminds us that we are connected to an essential energy—a force of wisdom and compassion—that is constantly being renewed. Look for the helpers, as Mister Rogers said. Notice them inside and outside.

15

The Burning World

Months after he attained enlightenment, the Buddha delivered what came to be called his Fire Sermon on a hilltop in India. He spoke to a thousand ascetics who, he knew, were used to performing daily fire sacrifices. The Buddha set out to blow their minds. Everything in this world is on fire, he told these newly converted monks. Including us. Our eyes, ears, noses, tongues, touch, and finally, our conscious minds—all of our faculties burn with craving or aversion or illusion for things and experiences that are impermanent.

Detachment is the way to peace and freedom, he taught. It is easy to picture that crowd of newly minted monastics nodding in rapt agreement. Even before they came to the Buddha, they were ascetics. Yes, of course, they would be all too happy to escape this burning building of a life. But what about the rest of us?

Some who heard the Fire Sermon, it is said, became fully enlightened on the spot. This kind of thing was often reported to have happened after the Buddha spoke. Was this true? I could easily picture monk scribes adding these juicy little postscripts to the sermons to underscore the power of the Buddha's teaching. I am sure that the

Buddha moved those who came to see him by his presence as well as by his words. He is portrayed as radiant, noble in bearing, serene—the embodiment of freedom and compassion.

But human beings are human beings. As remote as those ascetics are from us, they had the same parts. They had hearts and bodies and minds, each with habits of their own. They had an enlightened moment, I am sure of it, letting go of painful old stories and limiting beliefs to bask in the emanation of a new kind of love and freedom. But down the road, inevitably, there was at least a little more work to do, patterns to see, wounds to let heal.

Seeing the deep truths of life takes time and a certain willingness to be in the dark of not knowing. According to the ancient stories, the Buddha sat under the bodhi tree for forty days and nights. Whether this number can be taken literally or not, it still indicates a lot of calm seeing of past lives, old stories, and beliefs.

I'm not aware of anyone ever describing the Buddha's vowing to sit in the forest alone until he awakened as an act of grieving, but grief had to be part of the experience. He had turned his back on his wife and child and the life he knew. We can imagine how he felt by drawing on the times we have left places and relationships and jobs or have been left. He, like us, had to have grieved for bonds that turned out not to be permanent, for certainties that turned out not to be true.

His willingness to sit there and know this suffering became the ground of his great insight. We suffer because we cling to things that are burning, changing, passing, he realized. But this suffering, too, passes. And darkness, as the Buddha saw, ultimately gives way to the light of the morning star.

Detachment doesn't necessarily mean turning our backs on life. It can mean being with life as it is instead of staking our happiness on particular outcomes. Renunciation can mean loosening the grip of our attachments, opening the lens of our seeing so that our loved ones and our own lives can unfold in ways that can surprise us. In real life, I have learned, letting go doesn't mean shutting down or giving up. It can mean vowing to be aware and present, guided not by a fixed goal but by an intention to be compassionate, caring, and curious moment by moment.

Nora Ephron offered an example of this in a book that few would label spiritual: *I Feel Bad about My Neck*. Back in the day, she observed, people took the attitude that babies were babies. They would each have their own tendencies and ways of unfolding. You did the best you could—throwing balls, reading stories. But you understood that babies would turn out the way they would turn out.

"Suddenly, one day, there was this thing called parenting. Parenting was serious. Parenting was fierce. Parenting was solemn. Parenting was a participle, like going and doing and crusading. . . . Parenting was not simply about raising a child, it was about transforming a child."[14]

All beings are heirs to their own karma, taught the Buddha. We can love our children and the other people in our lives. We can love ourselves. Yet we can't control how things will unfold for them or for us.

Unexpected things will happen at unexpected times. They and we will get burned. What can we do in such a world? We can pay attention and be kind, even when our hearts are breaking. Especially then.

T. S. Eliot titled the third section of his great poem *The Wasteland* "The Fire Sermon." The poem describes the moral and spiritual desolation of London after World War I.

"The wind crosses the brown land unheard," the poet writes. "The nymphs are departed."[15] Eliot's version of the burning world opens on the banks of the River Thames, strewn with trash, rats scurrying about. The party is over—whether the nymphs are real women who were reveling the night before or magical beings from a pagan England that is now past. The dream of England, for Eliot and so many others, was devastated by the war.

The Fire Sermon section of *The Wasteland* portrays the way sensual pleasures burn away, too, as do the illusions of happiness connected to those pleasures spun into stories by the mind. Detachment also means disillusionment, seeing through this endless process of grasping at the pleasures of the five senses and spinning stories of future happiness. But in the Buddha's teaching disenchantment does not mean the end of magic, as it does in Western rationalism. Waking up from the trance of desire—seeing how we are caught—is the beginning of new possibilities, true aliveness. It is only as we awaken from our dreams of what life should be like that true love becomes possible. True love, it turns out, is not romantic attraction but a capacity and a willingness to be with life as it is.

The world is burning, but we can begin to see by that fiery light. Unclenching the fist of desire begins to open us to the ground of our being. The name Adam in Hebrew originally referred to a human being, to all of us, and it was derived from *adamah*, "earth or ground." Our deepest, earliest inner voice is our wordless awareness of being alive here on earth. Sometimes it is accompanied by a feeling of our nothingness, which does not mean worthlessness but instead an awareness that we are not separate or exempt from the way things go here on earth.

Humble means "lowly," from the Latin *humus*, "earth or ground." We are of a nature to grow and age and die, just like all earthly things. But our innate earthiness or humility also means that we have a lot of company and support, including the earth herself. Bringing the attention out of the spinning mind and back to the body, to the living experience of the present moment, grounds us and opens us to a greater awareness of life.

"People are somewhat gorgeous collections of chemical fires, aren't they?" wrote Harold Brodkey in the story "Angel." "We are towers of kinds of fires, down to the tiniest constituencies of ourselves, whatever they are."[16]

Those tiny constituencies include our mitochondria, the little engines in the center of our cells, and smaller still, the molecules and atoms inside, whirling, pulsing little fires. Even on our worst day, we are vessels for combustion on so many levels, all the way back to the Big Bang. When we pause in all our doing to be still and bring our attention home to the body, we are drawing close to the fire of life.

We can observe this deep truth in our own lives: Things change. Life flows. When we dare to let go of thinking and trying to control our lives, when we dare to just experience the darkness of the unknown, we discover the light of another kind of awareness that is closer to the body and the heart, closer to life.

In Newgrange, in the east of Ireland, is the mysterious Neolithic monument older than the pyramids in Giza and Stonehenge built so that the light of the rising sun on the winter solstice floods the chamber. At dawn sunlight pours through an opening above the main entrance and illuminates a triple spiral carving on the front wall. And here's a new twist. In recent years, due to drought, more neolithic symbols have appeared around Newgrange, and undiscovered smaller but similar structures are being unearthed. It's extraordinary to think of beings practicing a religion that was based on patience. The Latin root of the word is *pati*, "to suffer." Being willing to just sit there and wait in the dark, quietly observing instead of jumping to mind-spun conclusions, they watched how darkness gives way to new light. Although those watchers wouldn't use the word, that observation is *dharma*, the lawfulness or deeper truth of life.

The light that can guide us to this deeper understanding is not necessarily visible to the eye. On September 11, 2001, there were a couple of great guide dogs, Salty and Roselle, who helped their blind partners and others down the stairwells of the World Trade Center to safety. Both were calm and steady of heart in the midst of falling debris and unimaginable sounds and fear. Roselle, who led thirty people to safety besides her master, went home and immediately began playing with another dog as if she had done nothing extraordinary.

Anything can happen at any time. Things and people, even huge skyscrapers, can disappear without warning. We recognize this great truth when terrible things do happen: war, mass shootings, accidents, personal betrayals. We see the stunned look on the faces of those who have lost loved ones without warning. We see the survivors who can't fathom what happened. Nothing much can be said at such a time. But attentive presence helps, and sometimes dogs.

I once watched a video clip of a brigade of gentle, highly trained golden retrievers being led into a center full of survivors of the mass shooting at the Pulse nightclub in Orlando, Florida. Those dogs came to help just by sitting down and being with these shattered people, just breathing, sharing their warm animal presence. The dogs wore little jackets, inviting people to pet them and hug them. Many of the dogs were veterans, having shown up at many places of national tragedy although you wouldn't know it by looking at them.

Even when people seemed lost in pain, these gentle dogs leaned in, literally leaning on people and sitting on their feet. It's easy to imagine how comforting that gentle presence would be, the sides of a soft, furry golden dog body rising and falling, soft dog eyes patiently looking at you, free of judgment and calculation. Just observing, responsive, present.

Our own body can be a guide dog or a comfort dog. In the midst of the great fire of life, it can be a refuge and support. Bringing our attention home to the living experience of the present moment grounds us and opens us to a greater attention. As silly as it may seem, we may even silently say to ourselves, "Good body, thank you for being there for me." Think of all the burning buildings your body has come through: breakups and firings and stress of all kinds. Shut your eyes and register how loyal the body has been to you through it all, quietly breathing, pumping blood, and working away. Sense how eagerly it responds to the gift of your own attention, how it relaxes in the light of your kind attention. Take in the generosity and loyalty of this poor, sweet body, the way it wordlessly forgives you for not noticing it and how happily it meets you when you do.

As long as it breathes, the body comes when you call. Even when it's tired or doesn't feel particularly good, it responds to the touch of attention. Imagine how you would treat an actual dog this good and loyal. You wouldn't dream of criticizing its hair or pointing out that it could stand to lose a few pounds. You would express simple love and gratitude. You would be attentive and kind, bringing fresh water, taking it out to play from time to time.

Everything in this world is on fire, including our own lives. There will be changes and losses and devastation. And yet, in the midst of it, we learn to loosen the grip of our grasping and dreaming and turn our attention to the body. We can touch the earth of our present moment experience and remember that we are part of a greater wholeness, that we are supported and accompanied by forces and resources beyond the reckoning of the thinking mind. We can touch the truth that even on our worst days, we belong to something greater than our spinning minds. In the midst of darkness, we see that there is also light.

Traveling by car is like watching life on a screen, wrote Robert Pirsig in *Zen and the Art of Motorcycle Maintenance,* his classic account of a motorcycle journey with his eleven-year-old son that is really an inquiry into values. "You're a passive observer and it is all moving by you boringly in a frame. On a cycle the frame is gone."[17]

The secret of motorcycle maintenance—and of living a life that has value—has to do with drawing our attention to the quality of what confronts us here and now. No matter what we are thinking about or doing, according to Pirsig, we can cultivate a double awareness. We can be attentive to our thoughts and the work we are doing, yet sensitive to the quality of what is happening, to what is unknown.

Sometimes life delivers a shock that gives us a taste of what it means to be open to quality. A diagnosis comes in—for ourselves or a loved one—or news of a death or an attack somewhere in the world. Suddenly a shared meal or a hug or a beautiful day takes on new meaning. We remember that we live surrounded by mystery.

"The only thing that we can know is that we know nothing, and this is the highest flight of human wisdom," writes Tolstoy.[18] Briefly, we are wise.

Sometimes, we shock ourselves. On Christmas Eve in Grand Central Station, I'd seen heavily armed National Guard troops and police officers surround a deranged old homeless woman who had pushed her shopping cart into the terminal to take shelter from a storm. She'd stood clutching a broken doll, looking bewildered as the officers poked through the possessions that were spread out on the ground around her. I noticed one young officer. His stance was stern, but he had a look in his eyes that was pitying and also self-questioning, as if he were watching himself and incredulous that all that training and readiness to face danger had come down to this particular moment. *Life can be like this*, I thought as I watched him. We can find ourselves behaving in ways we never dreamed we could, even when we have the best intentions.

That moment was just about the opposite of a glass of wine with a loved one in the French countryside. But it had quality. It had depth, surprise, feeling, meaning.

Allow yourself to remember a time in your life when a shocking incident made you all the more aware of yourself and your surroundings. A death or a birth, an act of war or a moment of great peace— witness the way that sudden jolt of awareness opens us to the true richness and beauty of life.

PART FOUR

The Whole Truth

Sooner or later, greater understanding appears.
Flashes of insight come, but real understanding
takes time. It is an unfolding of awareness that
unveils qualities of acceptance and compassion.
Real wisdom is lived, not just thought. It requires
more of us, not just thinking but heart and wholeness and a capacity to let things be as they are. In
a state of greater presence, greater truths appear.

16

Butternut Goddess

The screen door banged as I sprinted across the yard to a butternut tree that had a limb at just the right height for pulling myself up. I hung by my knees from this perfectly placed limb, swung around backward and dropped to the ground, landing on my feet. I felt agile and capable every time I did this during my childhood, which was often.

"You always have to put your face in the lion's mouth," my mother said at the dinner table. "Always daring."

I was brave. But my mother said this like it was a bad thing, or a mix of good and bad. I was a little girl with a twin brother, shy but also "precocious," which was also mixed, meaning expressing myself in a way that was celebrated in little boys but a bit alarming in little girls: being outspoken with teachers, testing my courage and independence all the time. My mother's tone was warm but also weary, as if mine was a story all too well known. But I knew I was more than this! Like most children, I secretly felt capable of taking part in a much greater story, and the frustration of not being able to express this, the sadness of sitting at a table where people were just passing the potatoes and saying the same old words, locked away in their unseeing private worlds, caused me to run outside as soon as I could.

The tree seemed to welcome me. Her limbs were arranged just right for my size. After my spin and drop, I climbed back up, higher and higher. Sheltered by leaves that appeared faintly tropical, I looked down on a green world, feeling wild and good. Stretched out like an animal, breathing and listening to the breeze and the birds, I experienced life pouring in through every sense door. I felt that life was big and vast and full of possibility. What felt like anger and sadness and a wish to rebel inside the house was nothing but energy outside. And there was more. There was goodness in it, too, a wish to express the joy and possibility of being here.

That tree must have been young to have limbs so low. And yet when I visited my childhood home decades later I was shocked to find it gone, possibly due to a canker that is slowly killing the species. That shock revealed to me that this butternut was not just an object but a living being in my life. In her presence, I felt completely accepted, no part excluded—including my wildness. She was patiently and steadfastly there, and in her presence I felt part of the vast kingdom of creation.

In his instructions to those who wish to awaken, the Buddha encouraged them to go off by themselves and sit at the base of a tree, abiding peacefully away from the cares of the world. This detail is often treated as a relic from an ancient time when people spent more time outdoors. But I think it is a rich and relevant detail, since a tree sheltered and supported the Buddha during his awakening. According to legend it even burst into bloom to celebrate the event. And his instinct to take refuge under a tree was rooted in his own childhood memory. Once, the man who would become the Awakened One reached a point where he felt utterly desolate and lost. All his strenuous efforts to find liberation had led nowhere, it seemed to him, and he gave up, splitting off from his yogi friends, who considered him a quitter and a failure. The Buddha agreed and let go completely.

In the midst of this letting go, while lying on a riverbank, a heap of rags and bones, in the ashes of his dreams and aspirations, the Buddha remembered sitting under a rose apple tree as a little boy. That long-ago child wasn't doing or being anyone in particular. As his father and other men in the village plowed the fields as part of a planting festival, the little boy savored the joy and freedom of being completely alone in nature. The Buddha remembered that he had a body and a heart and an attention that was not thinking but seeing without judgment, receiving what arises the way that the butternut tree received me.

Our bodies, our portion of nature, resonate with nature. We can't help but see and sense and smell and breathe in life. When we go off by ourselves in nature or in some other quiet place, our hearts remember that life is a gift that is constantly being offered to us. We remember that we are not just a story in our head, urgent and dire as that story may seem. We are not just our painful self-judgments or dark thoughts. We are also part of a greater life and supported by larger benign forces. We tend to discover this when we let go and are like children, seemingly playing at life.

The butternut tree does not have one gender, growing male and female blooms—the female flower yields the nut. Yet my particular tree was maternal, as strange as this would have sounded to me as a child: a tree like my mother at her motherly best. Not every tree struck me as feminine—or masculine, for that matter—but that slender butternut played the role of Goddess of Compassion, holding me in her calm embrace, inviting me to explore my life, assuring me that I was a child of nature.

I had no conscious connection at that time to the idea of the divine feminine in any guise, not even to Mother Earth. We had a boat and camped and liked the outdoors well enough, but no one around me spoke of the earth as a being. We didn't go in for mysticism of any kind. I remember pining to be Roman Catholic instead of Methodist because Catholicism seemed so exotic, imbued with magic and incense and statues of Mary and many saints. I was mildly interested in the Greek goddess Artemis (the Roman Diana) because she was the twin sister of the brilliant Apollo, but she seemed both too remote and too human.

And yet as a child, I experienced something that would take me years to rediscover: the body is vast. When we let go of who we *think* we are and just sense how it feels to be here, alive and breathing, we remember that the body is not separate from life, but open to it and nourished and supported by it. Air comes in and out; we feel the sun on our skin and smell grass and receive countless other impressions. We are inextricably connected to life, the way trees are connected to each other through networks of fungi filaments.

In *The Overstory*, Richard Powers says, "The bird and the branch it sits on are a joint thing."[19] I had no such ideas at eight years old—but I experienced it. I felt different outside than I did inside, and especially when I climbed the tree. Lacking words for the experience, I used imagination as an extension of my senses and the feelings that flowed from them, exploring the sense of kinship I felt with wild nature.

I pretended I was a wild child living in a primordial forest in India. I knew all the plants and trees in the jungle and communicated with all the animals in their own languages. I was especially close to a superintelligent and superstrong black panther I named Striker. He was my best friend and protector, communing with me telepathically. Like me, Striker could turn invisible and teleport, and sometimes I could become Striker or he could become me. He was kind and gentle, but if necessary, he could kill. Inexplicably, Striker and I were both also highly trained, James Bond–like spies. When asked to by the U.S. government, we would teleport to various European capitals, undertaking missions too delicate and dangerous for anyone else.

Undoubtedly, Mowgli, the boy raised by wolves in Rudyard Kipling's *The Jungle Book*, played a role in this fantasy game, as did Bagheera, the wise black panther who counseled and protected the boy. (It's wonderful to think that I was indirectly inspired by the Indian Jataka Tales, stories of the lives of the Buddha before his enlightenment, including animal lives, since Kipling admitted to helping himself to them.) I was also clearly inspired by secret agent 007. But like all children at play, I was an artist using the materials close at hand. The story I acted out was deeply and truly mine. It was about the wild nature of life, that it was fluid not fixed. I flowed freely from little girl to jungle boy to jungle princess and on occasion to panther to international spy, from visible to invisible, from India to northern New York to Berlin. As a little kid I was kept in bounds by adults, but I didn't feel limited. And in the imaginary game that flowed from my sensations and feelings, in the vastness of the jungle and in my global spy network with my ability to teleport, I was unlimited.

Like all beings living closer to nature, First Australians understand that we live in a web of interconnection. They see that past and future, including the distant past and distant future, exist in the present moment. The author P. L. Travers, who grew up in Australia, once wrote that all children have aboriginal hearts. They also have aboriginal bodies and minds, and so do adults. Under everything poured into us by our culture and education, there is a capacity to return to our origins. Our body is our original home and a gift from our distant ancestors. Bringing our attention home to the moment-by-moment life of the body, our breath and sensations, roots us in life, quietly leading on to deeper feelings and essential truths.

The word *imagination* comes from an ancient root that means "to copy or imitate." When I played a jungle game, I believed I was doing more than just trying on roles from books and movies. The game followed the wisdom of the body and felt experience. I was exploring the fluidity and interconnection of life.

"Something marvelous is happening underground, something we're just learning how to see," writes Richard Powers in *The Overstory*. "Mats of mycorrhizal cabling link trees into gigantic, smart communities spread across hundreds of acres. Together, they form vast trading networks of goods, services, and information."[20]

Science is slowly rediscovering what ancient people knew. It is known that trees are more than separate objects that happen to give us oxygen and absorb carbon dioxide. They are linked and constantly communicate, helping each other in the face of their challenges. And more. Like the tree the Buddha sat beneath at his awakening greeting him and blooming for him, there is some scientific evidence now that trees really may be able to sense our presence, emitting fragrances and even changing shape slightly in response to us. This suggests that they aren't just communicating with each other. They are aware of us, too.

Our bodies can sense what people once knew when they lived more attuned to nature. Our hearts, which ancient cultures held to be the seat of consciousness, still know how to open to the world around us, to feel wonder and love. Deep down, under all the words and stories, we know we are not alone here. Usually, our thinking takes up all the attention, endlessly repeating what we believe we know. It doesn't trust that the body and the heart can discern essential truths. But in a time of overwhelming uncertainty, even confirmed atheists may find themselves looking up at the sky and the trees, thinking, "Help me."

In times of crisis, there is often an instinct to be alone, to sit quietly or go walking outside, feeling our feet on the ground and space all around. The body innately seeks contact with the earth because we are part of the earth. It senses the life that is being offered to us moment by moment, literally breathing it in through every sense door. It knows innately how to open to a greater world. And given enough time, the heart also opens, feeling the inexpressible preciousness of what the body senses, revealing another kind of mind under our ordi-

nary thinking mind, a mind that loves what it sees and feels part of it.
At such times, we stop being what the Australian Aboriginals call line
people and become like children who haven't forgotten the Goddess,
who may reside in a butternut tree.

According to legend, the boy who would be the Buddha pretended to sleep under that long-ago rose apple tree. Once his minders
went off to watch the plowing festivities, he sat up and crossed his legs
in meditation posture to experience the joy of solitude, the joy of not
needing to defend himself or acquire anything, the joy of being no one
in particular, just open, flowing experience. As a little girl, I too was
exploring how it felt to be fluid, not fixed, not separate but part of life.
Remembering the tree that supported and inspired me, I realize that
I was actually being helped to an essential truth. I was invited to experience being part of something wondrous and mysterious and vast.
I got to feel what it is like to be free from separation, not in control of
life but in harmony with it, adding my perspective and various pretend skills of spy craft, jungle knowledge, teleportation, and whatnot
to the very real experience I had of life. I imagined what it can mean
to serve, to have my life and expression come from a sense of connection. What else could that butternut be but a goddess, a messenger
from a greater world?

Dark times happen. Periods of bewilderment, of being lost in the
dark, are human. It can be a great comfort to remember that our
greatest spiritual stories, including the story of the Buddha and Jesus
of Nazareth and Moses, all include chapters about these figures ven-
turing out into the darkness of the unknown. The Buddha, for example, left family and home, teachers and friends—all that was familiar
and comfortable—to sit in the forest in the dark. He sat for forty days.
He was waiting, watching his mind states come and go, not knowing
what this would bring. We are told that Jesus spent forty days in the
desert. Moses spent forty years wandering in the wilderness. While

scholars believe that the forty in these instances is not a literal number, it clearly means a good long while.

Allow yourself to relax and remember a time when you felt lost, unsure of what would come. Remember how strange life seemed, but also relax into the realization that this is a human experience. It does not mean that you personally did something wrong. It means that you are human. The root of *bewilderment* means "to be in the wilderness" like Moses. Our great stories are not just "out there." They point to experiences that are deeply encoded in us. We know how it feels to be lost. Deep down, we know what to do. As the U.S. Forest Service advises us when we get lost in the woods: Stop. Stay calm. Observe. Take shelter if you can. In the forest, that might mean under a mothering tree, as the Buddha found. But when we are emotionally lost, we can take refuge in qualities of heart: self-compassion, kindness, patience.

The Christian calendar includes a time called Advent. Advent comes from the Latin word *adventus*, which means "coming." It is a time of opening to the darkness of the unknown, which in many traditions, including Buddhism, is the very definition of faith. Real faith, it turns out, is a willingness to be present to what is, instead of clinging to a story with a fixed conclusion. What will come? We don't know! But what if we faced the unknown surrounded by noble friends? Not just real friends who share your wish for a greater *wholeness* and *aliveness*. (The words don't really matter—we wish for a presence beyond words.) What if we allow ourselves to imagine how it would feel to call on great and good beings to accompany us? This can be great beings known or unknown, human or nonhuman—the Buddha, Jesus, Tara, Totoro, or, why not, that beautiful flowering bodhi tree that sheltered the Buddha during the long, dark night that preceded his awakening.

Don't be shy. Allow yourself to picture sitting under that wonderful tree—or climbing up into the lap of the Buddha. Let yourself pray for help from Tara or Mary, and imagine how it feels to be held in vast and unconditional love. In the midst of allowing ourselves to feel nurtured and accompanied in this way, it might occur to you that as hard and mysterious as life is, it is also full of benevolent forces. Most of us spend so much of our time imagining that we are all alone, surrounded by cruel and indifferent forces. But our times of darkness and bewilderment have always passed. Allow yourself to remember how life went on. What happened after that loss or heartbreak? Note any unexpected good things that came along, including the discovery of new capacities for understanding or compassion or strength.

Allow yourself to write down some of your wildest dreams for your life. Write with abandon, until the essence of your deepest wishes begins to shine through.

Here, for inspiration, is C. S. Lewis, in *Mere Christianity*: "Imagine yourself as a living house. God comes in to rebuild that house. At first, perhaps, you can understand what He is doing. He is getting the drains right and stopping the leaks in the roof and so on; you knew that those jobs needed doing and so you are not surprised. But presently He starts knocking the house about in a way that hurts abominably and does not seem to make any sense. What on earth is He up to? The explanation is that He is building quite a different house from the one you thought of—throwing out a new wing here, putting on an extra floor there, running up towers, making courtyards. You thought you were being made into a decent little cottage: but He is building a palace. He intends to come and live in it Himself."[21]

17

Seeking Verity

Verity climbed down from the scaffold and stood with me, looking up at his work. I murmured something about how otherworldly the statue looked. "I look for something other when I carve
them," he said. "They're not connected to this world. They're in another place, in their heavenly robes." I was wearing the clothes of a
Brooklyn-based writer, but I was also looking for clues about how to
be above this world, connected to that "something other."

From 1988 until 1997, the British sculptor and master stone carver
Simon Verity directed the carving of the West Portal, also known as
the Portal of Passion, of the Cathedral of St. John the Divine in New
York. Assisted by six apprentices and after 1993 by Jean-Claude Marchionni, a master stone carver from France, Verity spent eight to ten
hours a day from spring until fall, up on that scaffold slowly carving a
procession of thirty-two matriarchs and patriarchs from the Old and
New Testaments.

Verity explained that these holy figures lead churchgoers through
the portal we stared up at just twice a year, on Easter and on the
Feast of St. Francis (when elephants and a glorious parade of animals

enter for blessing) in October. The great bronze doors, also engraved with scenes from the Old and New Testaments and the Apocalypse, are called the "Easter Doors."

But Verity explained that the portal he was working on and the cathedral itself are not just a random if interesting work of architecture covered with sculpted biblical metaphors. It is all a work of sacred technology. The portal is a great funnel, drawing people into a carefully designed sacred space and sending them out again, transformed from their contact not just by words and images, but by the finer energies that collect and circulate within. On Easter, churchgoers are led in by the biblical guides Verity carved to experience the miracle of the empty tomb, the highest truth, the deathless. I made an effort to maintain a journalistic detachment, but this touched me and spoke to the secret agenda. There was a higher truth that was an actual finer energy that could be felt, not just thought, and Verity knew it.

"In the thirteenth century people used geometry to describe God and the cosmos," said Verity. "They understood that we're all connected and that life is connected." I loved visiting the cathedral. I felt as if I were under a higher order in that vaulted space, mysterious but real. I remembered the amazement in the eyes of some of the animals as they entered through the vast bronze doors on the Feast of St. Francis. Since they have senses far more sensitive and acute than our own, I wondered if animals could feel the finer vibrations of the sacred, if they can sense true goodness the way they can sense fear. I wondered if Verity could sense these vibrations. These were questions I vowed to myself not to actually ask Verity, questions that might seem naive or as if I were a spiritual seeker rather than a professional journalist. These were cards to be held close as I observed the man.

Handsome, with thick, wind-tangled hair threaded with silver and a friendly, self-deprecating manner, Simon Verity wasn't otherworldly in any obvious outer sense. He was and is a busy and accomplished man with work in the Victoria and Albert Museum, the American Academy in Rome, and the private collections of King Charles III, Sir Elton John, and Lord Rothschild. Yet there was something otherworldly about him, or about his calling. His very name meant Truth, and he carved in stone. I pointed this out to him, noting that he might have heard it before. He laughed with good-natured agreement, adding that he had always had an interesting relationship with his name and that it probably did influence his decision to become a contemporary version of a medieval artisan.

All the way up to the Upper West Side from Brooklyn, I had been prepared to meet a different kind of man, someone in touch with his body, working in a practical physical way, yet who was in alignment with something beyond his own experience, with a vast body of tradition. I had the idea that what he did might be close to devotion. I risked saying this, reasoning that devotion had a secular meaning as well as sacred, and Verity didn't disagree. He felt a connection with the body of this church, with all those who helped build this vast space, with the bishops, deans, and pilgrims who worshiped here. He believed that even those who lived and worked nearby were part of the life of the cathedral.

In fact among these otherworldly beings he was carving were the faces of friends and neighbors of the cathedral. Verity's friend Naomi became the face of the Old Testament Naomi. A Tibetan woman in exile became the face of Hagar, while a member of the cathedral staff and the owner of the Hungarian Pastry Shop, the coffee shop across the street, became Jonah and Simeon. This made sense to me listening to Verity talk, especially after we crossed Amsterdam Avenue to the Hungarian Pastry Shop to buy coffee. There among the clusters of students and other locals sat Verity's stone carving partner Marchionni, who smiled and shook my hand. But it also made sense to me as a seeker of the sacred. The same presence or energy or power that transformed those lives might transform mine.

Verity and I settled on a bench near a biblical garden, looking up at the gigantic Gothic Revival cathedral, contending with Liverpool Anglican Cathedral for the title of largest cathedral in the Anglican Church, the fourth-largest Christian denomination in the world. St. John the Divine is a sacred space, Verity explained. Just as in medieval cathedrals, the proportions are intended to fill us with a sense of the presence of God.

I wanted to feel this presence. I had traveled here on one of those stirring blue-sky autumn days in New York when everything seems to be illuminated, beautiful, charged with impending change. It was 1994, in the middle of a decade of prosperity and innovation. I was a mother, a wife, a writer, living in a brownstone on a tree-lined street in Brooklyn, all seemingly solid and fortunate things. But I knew there was a heartbreak in the center of life. That day there were changing leaves edged with golden light, excited baby-faced students wearing bright new Columbia University sweatshirts—and no escaping the knowledge that life was fleeting and impermanent. Nothing stayed. "When people came together to build these extraordinary structures, there was a sense of everybody coming together for a common purpose," said Verity, who received some of his training at the beautiful medieval Wells Cathedral in England. "People were building blocks in a greater whole, and individual egos weren't so important. What I'm trying is part of this medieval tradition—working with a sense that we're all connected in a unified whole."

Verity spoke of how much he learned from the extraordinary people who visited the cathedral—just recently he had heard an amazing talk on the universe by the cosmologist Brian Swimme. A shadow passed over the garden as the sun slipped away. I sipped the hot coffee against the chill, liking Verity's easy openness and unpretentiousness yet disappointed with our talk, with myself, realizing that what I was seeking might not be found in any words he could say but in the quality of concentration I glimpsed in him as he worked on the scaffold.

"A real teacher teaches with his back," I heard once from a wise old painter and author I had interviewed not far from where Verity and I sat. The old man had heard it from a Zen master in a monastery in Japan, just after the last world war. I pictured the Japanese master walking upright and serene through a country devastated by war, demonstrating an inner stillness and steadfastness that didn't depend on what the Buddhists call "the eight worldly winds"—gain and loss, pleasure and pain, praise and blame, fame and disrepute: the up and down way things go. On his face, I envisioned gravitas and grace, the qualities Verity carved in the faces on the portal.

I wanted to know what Verity clearly seemed to understand in his body, with his hands: how to connect with a greater wholeness, how to be in alignment with something changeless beyond the rush of life that carries us along like leaves on a stream. My secret mission had to do with gathering clues about how to be more alive. I asked Verity if he actively felt a connection with a greater presence while he worked—not just thought about it but actually felt it.

"I've had moments of real connection with my work," said Verity. "I feel as if a spark has leapt and then it's gone. These moments aren't continuous. I keep trying to get more of a flow, to allow more without trying to control so much. How can we extend these moments of connection? That's the question and that's what's so painful. You have the sense of this opening, this other energy passing through, and it's utter bliss when it happens, but it's transitory. I think this is what any artist is searching for. What drives you on is that it's there and it's just a question of getting out of the way."

In the same way that meditators use the breath as an anchor of attention, he drew his attention to two square inches of limestone. "There's something in the repetitive action of the work," he said. "I'm hitting that stone once every second for two hours, and then I stop work for twenty minutes, and then I begin again, and for eight or ten hours a day, that's what I do. That's extraordinary, isn't it? And

I've been doing that for thirty years. And that's a very strange thing to be doing."

Life rushed on, but I never forgot what Simon Verity said about repeatedly hitting the stone. It took a long time for the true import to seep in, as if I were made of stone—and I was, in a way. As one inclined to big sweeping answers, to searching with my mind but not my body, the admission by this creator of otherworldly statues that he created them by bringing his attention down to small, simple, finite actions rang true, and like many true things it was hard to process—a code I had to learn to break on my own.

In 2004 Verity was commissioned to design and build a hand-carved map of the United Kingdom as part of the British Memorial Garden in New York's Hanover Square, commemorating the sixty-seven British victims of the September 11, 2001, attack on the World Trade Center. In the wake of this horrific evidence of the impermanence and unpredictability of life, many New Yorkers had discovered a version of Verity's truth.

Collectively for a time, people in the city practiced that small but momentous change of pulling the attention out of our usual state of distraction and bringing it to the present moment, to the sensation of being here, meeting other eyes and opening doors. We discovered it opened up everything. In that simple act, we invited the outside world in, the better angels of our nature, God. Time passed and people forgot, including me, but when I meditated or walked in the morning, I remembered. This is how you can feel connected to a larger life: focus on one finite task, two square inches of granite, one conscious breath, and you open to the infinite, to reality.

Very slowly over many years, I learned that consenting to be with what is, body, heart, and mind, without judging or seeking to change anything in any way, allows a new energy or vibration or feeling of life to appear—and this is the truth I was searching for. This truth can be found only in the moment. One moment we are fully embodied beings, sensing and feeling the world around us and inside us, opening to perceptions of reality that lead us toward a living unknown. The next moment, we contract into thought, into stories about who we are and what the world is like, splitting off from the whole to claim our little portion of the life force as our own. But from earliest childhood, that same energy in us seeks the greater energy, seeks to be part of the greater whole.

I slowly came to accept that the drama of being a self and being no self plays out over and over again without end. I remembered it happening from earliest childhood. I remembered one day in particular, a day that ultimately may have inspired me to seek Verity and the cathedral. Johnny and Joey, the boys from next door, rolled around in the ruins of my snow fort, oblivious to the devastation they wrought. Writhing around in shiny dark snowsuits with the hoods drawn up tight, barking and diving into each other, they seemed more like seals than humans. Suddenly and passionately, I knew who I was: I was not like them.

As a child I didn't think in terms like *ego* or *self,* but I knew the reality behind the labels. I knew the act of contraction, as if a fist were closing around a jewel, as if gates were drawing closed to protect a town, as if I were armoring myself against the world. One moment, I was being alive in the world, enjoying the hush and blue light inside my burrow, marveling how warm snow could be. The next moment I was crushed under stinging snow, then lying exposed and stunned under ice-colored sky. I was hurt and furious, but then suddenly sure I was not like them. One moment there was no self and then suddenly there was.

I remember going inside to play, to nurse and elaborate my sense of being special and not like Johnny and Joey. I padded around the living room in bare feet, pretending I was a princess in a primordial forest in India. The sense of self is born of contrast, and the living room after the snow felt like a jungle. I believed that I was not just an Indian princess in ancient times but also, inexplicably, an international spy who would often be summoned to various world capitals on a moment's notice. The sense of being a spy, of having a secret aim and identity, was both a product of the Cold War times I grew up in and an expression of an instinct that life could be deeper and richer and more meaningful. This was an instinct and a wish that would persist.

Children use their bodies, the whole of their sensate experience, along with their imaginations, to experience the world. The world is alive to them, full of surprising possibilities. But children are also engaged in that other drama. From the outside, I might have looked like an ordinary little white girl creeping around the living room of a brick ranch house in northern New York in the depths of winter. But I also sensed there was a life inside that was deep, wild, powerful, and connected to something vast. Like most children, I secretly sensed I was capable of very great efforts and deeds, like, say, carving otherworldly statues on great cathedrals. It would take me years, decades, to realize that connecting my energy with a greater energy came down to a simple repetitive action like being present and striking stone.

Later that day, I was taken skiing at a local hill, no doubt to stop me from climbing over the furniture talking to an invisible animal in what I hoped was a regal Indian accent. I loved the solitude of skiing, the way it let me be alone with what I preferred to think of as a mountain. I remember resting on my ski poles on top of the hill. The air had the cold metallic smell of coming snow. The sky was heavy with bruise-colored snow clouds, giving everything the hushed intimacy of a cathedral. Just for a moment, I felt that I was part of something exalted and marvelous.

I knew I was in a world that was vast and mysterious, but there was an order. I knew I did not know enough, that I needed to know more.

It would be many years before I discovered that what I needed to know was not to be found in some singular and extreme act of bravery or brilliance, but in the small repeated act of coming back to the present moment, letting go of who I think I am. As the stone carver Simon Verity told me, a connection with the infinite can appear in the midst of attending to something very finite. It can feel like doors swinging open, even like great bronze Easter Doors, allowing us to sense and feel how good it is to be here, creating a spark that can leap, as Verity said, into a wish to join a greater good.

The practice of presence takes resolve. But the resolution that is required is more willingness than will.

The Latin root of *resolution* is made of two parts—go back (*re*) and loosen (or *solution* in the sense of allowing our concentration to open and spread—to grow wider). Opening to a greater presence means reclaiming this ancient root meaning, understanding that we are meant to stop striving outward and grasping for solutions beyond ourselves, making instead a gentle U-turn to our own experience. Rather than a tight, narrow focus on what we think we need to change in our lives or fix in ourselves, we discover that we see more as we loosen up—opening the lens wide. We discover that seeing more requires compassion. We must offer ourselves—the whole of our experience—our kind acceptance. Let there be no orphans—no thoughts or feelings or memories of past deeds deemed too low or dark to be seen.

Experiment with self-forgiveness. When we are quiet, at the end of meditation or perhaps when we are out in nature or otherwise loose and relaxed, we can say "forgiven" to ourselves, like a mantra or prayer. For a moment or two as we practice this, we may feel ourselves emerge from the cage of our thinking into a warmer, more expansive awareness, an awareness that is more truly who we are than the stories and histories we cling to so insistently. Notice that this forgiveness practice is calming and grounding. It is not self-indulgent. It is not giving ourselves a pass for everything we have done or left undone. It is a gesture of recognizing and accepting our full humanity. It is humbling, pulling us out of our heads and returning us to the earth.

Not surprisingly, the word *forgive* comes from a word that means "to give." To forgive a debt is giving freedom to ourselves or another—loosening the shackles, lifting a burden. Self-forgiveness is giving in advance. It is being loving and generous with ourselves. Just for a moment, experiment with how it feels to be granted forgiveness in advance. In other words, widen your heart and your view to encompass the whole of you—peaceful, reactive, spacious, contracted, angry, sad, full of joy. Remember that the Buddha taught that enlightened or not, challenges will continue to arise here on earth. Things will go awry sometimes, and sometimes not. And you are lovable and welcome here on earth.

Notice that self-forgiveness is really giving yourself up to be seen just as you are, undefended and vulnerable—every part of you, your courage and fear, your fineness and times of faltering and holding back. Notice how it feels to be willing to be fully human—and held by a spacious awareness that is compassionate and wise beyond words.

18

Finding the Path

A mong the tasks or "yogi jobs" a participant can volunteer for
during silent retreats at the Insight Meditation Society, a Buddhist meditation center in rural Massachusetts, the most resonant
in every sense is that of bell ringer. Before dawn and before every
meditation session during the day, the bell ringers walk around the
grounds and through the halls of a rambling brick building that was
once a Jesuit seminary, striking a bronze bell that is held suspended
by a thick strap. I remember being curled in a little cell of a room,
hearing the bell sound deep and low in the distance. As the "awak-
ener" progressed on his or her appointed rounds, layer upon layer of
reverberations built up so that the ringer literally struck a chord that
touched the heart—at least this heart.

I remember walking to the meditation hall with others as the
bell sounded, feeling as if I were being led out of a wilderness onto an
ancient path. It was as if the bell were a torch that had been passed
from the distant past to lead me out of the isolation of my ordinary
thought toward a greater awareness. The contemporary Vietnamese
Zen master Thich Nhat Hanh spoke of waking the bell so that it can

call us to our true home. We wake each other, I found on that retreat. But the home I felt called to was not a fixed abode—even a "divine abode," which is the common English translation for the finer emotional states of friendliness, compassion, joy, and equanimity. I came to feel as if I were remembering another way of abiding with life, inwardly as well as outwardly. My true home turned out to be the fluid state of seeking and following the path to awakening.

"I had been my whole life a bell, and never knew it until I was lifted and struck," writes Annie Dillard in *Pilgrim at Tinker Creek*.[22] According to discourses found in both the Theravada school's Pali canon and some of the *agamas* in the Chinese Buddhist canon, the Noble Eightfold Path, the way to awakening and liberation, was not invented but rather rediscovered by Gautama Buddha. I think people from different times and cultures approach spiritual practice in different ways. At least I was influenced by the American ideal of the rugged individualist. Since the Insight Meditation Society is in rural Massachusetts, I often prepared for its rigors by thinking of Henry David Thoreau, who lived alone for two years, two months, and two days in a tiny cabin at the edge of Walden Pond. "I went to the woods because I wished to live deliberately, to front only the essential facts of life," he wrote.[23] I went on retreat because I desperately wanted to know what it means to be alive. But I went believing that one should be self-sufficient and wary of following anyone else's path.

I was mindful that when Thoreau wrote about leaving Walden, he mused about how quickly a path can be worn in the earth and in the mind: "How worn and dusty, then, must be the highways of the world, how deep the ruts of tradition and conformity!"[24] Somehow I missed the forest of Thoreau's message for the romance of living in a little cabin among the trees. For Thoreau follows that burst of American individualism by concluding that when a person moves in the direction of living a more real and essential life, "new, universal, and more liberal laws will begin to establish themselves around and within him. . . . In proportion as he simplifies his life, the laws of the universe will appear less complex, and solitude will not be solitude, nor poverty poverty, nor weakness weakness."[25] It took a long time for me to register that at Walden, Thoreau found a way to abide peacefully with life—a way to live in which he was not independent and alone, but part of a greater wholeness. Through voluntary simplicity, he had found a path to a greater way of living, a path to truth.

As moved as I was, I didn't volunteer to be a bell ringer, signing up only for group jobs like pot washer or floor cleaner, seeking to be a worker among workers, another pair of hands, although I knew that ringing the bell was really a group activity also. A friend who volunteered told me he wasn't just waking others, but himself and also the bell. We wake each other. We offer the path the living material of our own lives. We bring the path to life.

Yet I saw how quickly a moment of open awareness would attach to memories, images, and thoughts—how quickly it would be enlisted in the cause of being a particular special "someone." *Best not to inflame this tendency even further by taking on an auspicious spiritual role*, I thought. In college, I had read a novel based on Dante's *Inferno*, about a young African American man making his way through various hellish American cities. One image stayed with me: the young man at the end of a bar, hiding a secret purity under a ratty old coat and a cool look. For a long time, I treated being on retreat as if I were in a rough bar. I acted as if I thought it best to keep my deepest wish and my full human nature under wraps. To risk following the one was to risk exposing the other.

I misunderstood what the Buddha meant when he told his monks to abide "independent, not clinging to anything in the world." This was not without basis. One becomes so sensitive during a silent retreat that a harsh or indifferent glance can slice right through you, just like the bell. But slowly I learned the truth of what Thich Nhat Hanh said:

"But just as the suffering is present in every cell of our body, so are the seeds of awakened understanding handed down to us from our ancestors." I began to understand that the true independence isn't individuality, which is clinging to self (if only for protection), but falling more deeply into life and into my true humanity.

For a long time, I thought I had to go it alone. But one day I took my seat in the meditation hall and, looking around at the others, was amazed and touched that so many of us had managed to come so far to be together—and not just from New York or California or even South Africa but through all kinds of difficulties and challenges. And all of this common effort was made to be quiet together and try for a greater awareness, unattached to particular memories or thoughts or feelings, free from being a particular someone. Wrapped in shawls or yoga blankets, sitting still with backs straight on cushions, we looked like the earliest humans, at least as I thought of them. We were also like early humans in the sense of being like children again, who seem to open to reality with their whole beings.

At first, turning the attention to essential facts of life in such conditions, to the body and the breathing, felt huge and daunting, like descending into a vast cave full of unexplored forces with just a dim flickering light. Yet, I had the sense that if I just kept going, I might come upon wonders. And over time wonders were revealed, chief among them the light of conscious awareness or mindfulness itself. Although it often seemed as if it wasn't much brighter than a night light, I came to realize that it was the strongest force in me because unlike other parts and attachments that changed, this light seemed to be independent of outside circumstances, clinging to nothing in this world. It was amazing to discover that this little light of mindfulness—and my intermittent search for greater awareness and true liberation—turned out to be my truest home, what was most abiding.

According to Zen master Dogen, the path to awakening and liberation is not a line but a circle. When we sit down to remember the light of mindfulness, when we sit down to meditate or otherwise seek to awaken to what is truly abiding, we are joined by the Buddha and awakened ones from ancient times. I felt enormously supported on retreat, and I began to wonder if the Buddha's rediscovery of the path might not have been an extraordinary act of remembering that came to benefit beings in all times.

Smṛti in Sanskrit, *sati* in Pali, and *Drengpa* in Tibetan—all these words mean "to remember," and they point toward a quality of understanding and living that draws on our whole being. To "re-member" or "re-collect" means to have the head and heart and body all in alignment, all gathered, concentrated, and calmed. I realized that Thoreau must have discovered this state, which the Buddhists call *samādhi*, when he described in his journals being in accord with nature, his mind like a lake untouched by a breath of wind, his life in "obedience to the laws of his being." In a state of samādhi, the Buddha rediscovered the path to full awakening and liberation.

The Eightfold Path of the Buddha contains eight steps or trainings: right view or understanding, right intention or thought, right speech, right action, right livelihood, right effort, right mindfulness, right concentration—culminating in a higher understanding and intention. Bhikkhu Bodhi writes that what is commonly translated as "steps" is better described as components or strands, "comparable to the intertwining strands of a single cable that require the contributions of all for maximum strength."[26] Many Buddhist teachers substitute the translation "right" with "whole" or, sometimes, "recollected." When we are in a state of inner alignment, when we are mindful, it is natural to live in a way that is more sensitive and resonant with the life around us, where nongrasping and nonharming are not a kind of poverty or weakness but nobility.

In outside life there is no bell, no sitting with allies in a big hall, no stillness in which to come upon a calm lake or explore a cave. There are storms. It can seem frustratingly circular, that the first step on the path is right understanding. It seems that all on our own, we are to come to an understanding that consists of two main strands—that all our actions have consequences and that there is no inherently fixed self.

Yet there are openings. In the wake of a hurricane, for example, we lost power for four days. I collected sticks in the yard to burn as kindling in the woodstove and hauled buckets of water into the house to flush the toilet and wash the dishes. I performed these actions in a slow and unpracticed way. My true vulnerability, my true lack of connection inside and outside, was suddenly painfully exposed. I saw, again, that I am a collection of parts, of thoughts and dreams, and that I am at the mercy of forces outside my control.

And yet I saw that this very act of seeing, of surrendering to what is and really noticing the state of affairs, brought a new understanding. A quality of mindfulness appeared that was quicker and more sensitive than my usual thought. You might say I pulled myself together. I became aware that a house grows dark and cold at night without someone to build a fire and tend it and that it's good to wake up to a cup of coffee and a tidy house. I became the hearth keeper, the matriarch. I saw that while I was clearly no one special at these chores, I was engaged in something useful.

It takes a long time to cook over a fire—hours! Yet this was not an inconvenience but the center of the evening. The light and warmth from the fire, the promise of warm food, the common talk of how it was coming along, and the stories as we ate—as all of this unfolded, I realized there is always another possible way of living, a way of relating mindfully to what is elemental and crucial. I also saw that you can give yourself to a task in a way that makes it an act of generosity and at the same time a means of inner search for connection. Tending the stove, I realized that what the Buddha taught may actually be possible to realize, because we and our ancestors are not separate. They live on in us in the rhythm of our breathing, in the light of mindfulness, in our capacity to open to what is. They accompany us when we seek to remember.

The path begins with a single step.

Mindfulness is a movement of return to the present moment. It is an action of remembering—not a memory of the past, but a direct and wordless experience of presence. Mindfulness is not a thought, but rather attention itself. It is open and without agenda. Sometimes, it is compared to peripheral vision.

Yet at the same time, mindfulness is remembering. It is that gentle tug or the wordless call we feel to be more present, to stop missing our real purpose here, which is to really be here. Mindfulness is not an answer to suffering in the sense of being an intellectual formula that will help us skip over difficult feelings and experiences. It is the energy of awareness that allows us to see and participate in reality, to be with what is arising in a way that is compassionate and open.

The root of *educate* is *educare*, which means "to bring to wholeness." Mindfulness educates us by bringing us to a greater wholeness. Moments of mindfulness show us that we are more than our most painful reactions and feelings, more than what has happened to us—we are also an observing presence that is connected to a greater wholeness.

No matter what is happening, we can remember to be present. A Pali word, which is translated into English as "mindfulness" is *appamāda,* which literally means "nonnegligence" or "absence of madness." When we find ourselves lost in thought, distracted and anxious, longing for something we can't name, we can come home to presence. We can rest in a caring attention that remembers that we are more.

19

Spinning Straw

Once a poor miller was summoned to meet with a king. The sum-mons alone must have filled him with terror. Evolutionary bi-ologists tell us that we are wired to link survival with acceptance by the tribe. And this king was the absolute ruler of the miller's tribe, holding the power of exile, life, and death.

The poor miller trudged to the palace as if headed to his execu-tion. The king surprised him by asking about his family, probably con-gratulating himself on his noble kindness and expansiveness, to be able to broach such a personal question with a subject who could not speak unless bidden. Startled and desperately eager to please and to be deemed acceptable, so it seemed even to the miller as he spoke, he answered that he had a beautiful daughter with golden hair. But this sparked not one flicker of interest in those cold, royal eyes. The miller saw that his precious daughter, his treasure, meant nothing to the king. She was just another pretty woman to a man surrounded by pretty women—no one special, an object really, easily replaceable.

The miller blurted that his beautiful, golden-haired daughter could spin straw into gold. The Brothers Grimm reported that he made this wild claim to seem important, and this is true. But the roots went deeper. The miller knew that he himself was no one in the eyes of the king, just a minor problem to be solved, an impediment to the flow of tax revenue into the royal coffers. But his daughter was special. The miller's love for her was sacred in the deep sense of set apart from the muck and disappointment of his life. He saw how unique she was in this world, how good and beautiful. He wanted this king to appreciate the marvel of her existence, and he knew this king loved gold.

We can only imagine how the poor miller felt after he spoke. He had betrayed what he most deeply loved and understood to be true. He loved his work and he loved his daughter. Milling grain is one of the most ancient human occupations. Even hunter-gatherer societies had millers. It is hard, humble work, but it is wholesome, even holy. The miller helped feed people, grinding the grain for their daily bread. How he wished that he stood before the king calm in the knowledge that it was good to be a miller, even noble in the root sense of taking care of kin, but at least good enough. Yet it was worse. He had forgotten that it was good enough to be a father of a daughter, and that she was enough, magic enough, just as she was.

Now it was too late. "This is a skill that would serve me well," said the king. "Bring your daughter to the castle in the morning, and I will put her to the test." He didn't have to warn the miller that hiding such a treasure would lead to death for them both. The miller didn't sleep that night. The next morning, he brought his daughter to the palace. Sorrowfully, apologetically, he tried to explain what had happened but soon faltered. He could find no explanation beyond his inner smallness, no context beyond a fear-driven reaction. He had betrayed his beloved daughter, betrayed a love he held sacred. He remembered holding her when she was a baby. He watched the guards lead her away into a royal dungeon piled high with straw.

The king swept into the cell. The miller's daughter was pretty, he observed. Her blond hair and tawny skin glowed, and her clear blue-gray eyes looked out at the world with forthright innocence and bright intelligence. But this was not the point. He gestured to the wheel and spindle set up in the center of the room. "Let's see if your father tells the truth," he said. "Spin this straw into gold by dawn tomorrow or you die."

Most of us know the version of the story told by the Brothers Grimm, who collected it in Germany in 1812. But other versions of this tale stretch back four thousand years, and many of us have spoken of spinning straw into gold. Most humans know how it feels to be in this impossible situation, desperate to spin something shiny and golden, full of the doomed sense that we must do something incredible, must do more and be more than we really are.

The miller's daughter sat alone in her cell, plucked from an ordinary life that now seemed impossibly happy. She could think of no way out. She began to weep, abandoning herself to bottomless sorrow and fear. Finally, as her crying subsided, a door opened and a strange little man appeared.

"Good evening, fair maiden," he said. "Why do you weep so bitterly?"

He smiled, tipping his head and looking at her quizzically. Although he was tiny, he looked almost handsome, pale with an aquiline nose. But he did not meet her gaze for long. A nervous tic pulled his smile into a wincing grimace, and his eyes blinked rapidly. He seemed to be calculating very rapidly. Who was he? Where did he come from and what did he want? In ordinary conditions, she might have asked such questions. But her life was on the line.

"I'm supposed to spin all this straw into gold by morning or I'm dead," she said. "I have no clue what to do."

"What will you give me if I spin it?" He smiled, as if this question were a joke, as if he were far too kind to take advantage of her. But the smile became a wince. She immediately took off her necklace and offered it to him. No, no, he said softly, holding up pale hands with long, thin fingers. His way of speaking and his gestures were overly careful, as if he were walking on ice. She held out the necklace, insisting, and his pale hand darted out quickly and snatched it, a lizard capturing a fly.

He sat down at the huge spinning wheel, turning his back to her. Fishing a notebook and pen out of his worn jacket, he made feverish calculations. He rubbed his forehead, studied what he wrote, blinked rapidly. *Whir, whir, whir*, the wheel spun round. For a long time nothing happened, then the spindle glinted with threads of gold. Amazed, the miller's daughter asked him what he was doing. He shrugged his sharp, thin shoulders and mumbled that it was science, not magic. What kind of science, she wanted to know. She wanted to talk with him, to know him, but a cold, detached look warned her away.

The strange little man spun all night until all the straw was gone. The faint smell of sun and earth that came in with the straw was also gone, and the cell grew damp and cold. The first rays of sunlight struck piles of golden string. The miller's daughter leaned closer to see the last of his work. She rested her hand on his shoulder.

Startled, he looked up into her eyes and felt a surge of joy. He saw himself reflected there in sparkling points of light. After a lifetime in the shadows, invisible to everyone in the palace, tolerated only for his skill at calculation (and they asked such silly questions; they had no idea what he could do), he was seen. He existed. A beautiful woman thought that he was marvelous. Bowing deeply, happy, he slipped away.

The king was delighted with the gold, but this only fueled his greed. The miller's daughter was led into a larger cell with an even bigger pile of straw. Again, she was commanded to spin all of it into gold by dawn or be killed. Again, she despaired and wept, and again the door opened and the little man appeared.

"How did you know?"

He shrugged and smiled his wincing smile. "I know this king."

She took the ring from her hand and offered it to him. "My mother's ring," she said. He waved it off, but again his hand darted out and took it from her. He tucked it into his pocket, turned his back on her, and sat down at the wheel. The deference and smiles were gone. He checked his calculations and bent to his task. Straw went in and gold spooled out. "How did you learn this magic?" His body cringed from the question. "There is no such thing as magic," he said. "Magic is what people call science because they can't do the math."

For a flash, she saw his real deformity, what kept him from love. It wasn't his tiny size but the way his mind, his math, held himself apart from life. She asked him what his science taught him about how to live. He looked up and studied her, eyes narrowed. "When you do the math and learn the vastness of the cosmos, you have no patience for anyone who insists they are special in any way."

How self-enclosed he seemed to her, cringing away from her as he spoke. "Have you ever been afraid that you might die?" she asked. His smile froze on his face. His curse was to go on living on and on without really living. "Suddenly you see that everything is special, every moment."

By first light, the room was full of gold and the little man was gone. The greedy king was overjoyed. She was not surprised when he led her into a still larger cell full of even more straw. "I know," she said. "I must spin all to gold or else . . ."

"And you will be my bride," the king said as if he were giving her the greatest gift of all.

"I have nothing left to give you," she later said to the little man. By now, she saw how bitter and full of rage he was, how full of calculations and dreams and empty of life. She herself had neither magic nor math. She was nothing but herself, as plain as straw.

"Give me your firstborn child if you become queen," the little man said quickly. Was he serious? The miller's daughter saw the hatred and grasping in his eyes. She felt a surge of anger. She had asked for none of this, not her father's damning praise, not the king's imprisonment, nor marriage to that tyrant who was willing to see her dead. She said yes to the horrible little man's outrageous demand. None of this was her choice, none of it felt real.

The little man bent to his work. He looked very old to her, and yet as wizened and otherworldly as a newborn. He had lived a long time but only in his mind. She shivered to think of it. The hours passed in silence; the wheel turned; the smell of earth and sun ebbed away as straw became gleaming coils of gold. At last, the little man stood. He knew the miller's daughter would marry the king. His face was pale. His smile was a wince. He despised her. She was just like all the others he had loved and helped. They always left in the end. "Don't forget your promise," he said and slipped away.

The king kept his vow. Their marriage was a fairy tale in the grimmest sense: lavishly beautiful and dark. But then a child came, and she discovered a love that was pure and unbounded. She took the baby in her arms and showed it life, trees, sky, dogs, and cats. She took him out to the stables to see the horses. Holding her baby in her arms, breathing in the smell of sun-warmed hay, she felt a joy and ease she had never known. She felt as if she were a strand in the greater web of life.

Yet one day the little man reappeared to collect what he had been promised. Desperate to save her son, the young queen offered him riches, anything else in the kingdom. He shook his head no. "Something alive is dearer to me than all the wealth in the world." She knew he would say this. He of all people knew that life was more precious than gold. She wept. He felt a pang of compassion and gave her a distant chance.

"You have three days," he said. "Find out my name and you can keep your child." His compassion was veined with a rage to be known.

He was the one who had spun gold. He wanted the kingdom to know his name. All night, the queen lay awake thinking of names and of all she knew of the little man that might show her a way out. After hours of this, she went and gathered her child in her arms. The minute we try to save ourselves we are lost, she realized. Spinning thoughts, we forget the living experience of the present moment, forget the body and the heart that can help us remember our deepest humanity, that knows the true value of being alive. She stood in the darkness of a summer night, holding her child, feeling the warmth and weight of him, smelling his sweet baby smell. The moment felt sacred, yet not at all separate from ordinary life. She was no one, just a pair of arms, a witnessing consciousness. She was nameless, any mother who had ever lived holding her child in the middle of the night. And yet as humble as this embrace was, she felt that by enacting it she was taking her place in a line of mothers stretching back to the first mother. She was a human being. She felt as if she were taking her place in a great mystery.

The next morning, she summoned a messenger she could trust. Tall and calm, he seemed a very different helper than the nervous little spinner. He was there to listen and observe. The messenger set out and searched the kingdom, asking people about curious creatures with curious names. He visited cafés and marketplaces; he listened to people talking in the streets. He listened to everyone without judgment. On the morning of the third day, the messenger returned.

"Near the edge of a distant forest, I saw a little hut," he told her. "Outside the door before a roaring cooking fire, there was a wiry little man dancing and singing with wild abandon. 'Today I brew and tomorrow I bake,' he sang. 'Tomorrow the queen's child I'll take.' The little man cackled and stirred the pot. 'How sad that nobody will ever know that my name is Rumpelstiltskin.'"

Of course, thought the queen. The name literally means "little rattle stilt," a poltergeist or spirit that rattles the ridgepole of a house. It stands for the rage to knock the dishes off the shelves, to shock and awe, to be somebody special. The queen remembered her father's boast, her imprisonment, the desperate spinning, then her holding her baby in her arms. In this moment, she remembered who she really was.

She knew his name.

She saw how desperate he was to be known, to plant his flag, to make his mark. Yet being fully alive, she saw, took a kind of surrender. We must agree to take our place in life, to be what we actually are, body, heart, and mind. We must dare to be straw.

She would speak the truth. She would speak his name and let the whole kingdom know who spun the gold. She felt her feet on the earth and the warmth of the sun, felt her love for her son and freedom from all fear. He cocked his head expectantly, eyes blinking.

"Are you . . . Rumpelstiltskin?"

For a beat, the little man was silent. "A witch told you!" he screamed. He stamped his foot so hard that it sank into the earth. He pulled it with the full force of his rage, splitting himself in two. This didn't feel strange but almost reassuring, a terrible confirmation. He had always felt divided, trapped in his head, cut off from life. Howling, he pulled himself together and limped off, vowing to find someone better than a miller's daughter.

She watched, marveling that he had never asked her for her name, or the name of the son he wanted for his own. She was the miller's daughter, and now a queen. She smiled. She knew that ultimately she was no one, anyone, and part of everything.

"If you want your children to be intelligent, read them fairy tales," Albert Einstein is credited with saying. "If you want them to be more intelligent, read them more fairy tales."

How can reading fairy tales make us more intelligent? Fairy tales have ancient roots—*Rumpelstiltskin* is said to be four thousand years old after all. Yet a little reflection reveals that all good stories, particularly those we associate with children, are as old as humanity. They reveal our deepest human longings and hidden wisdom.

We can get trapped in our stories about who we are and what has happened to us. But the stories we encounter in childhood and beyond can also remind us that we are larger than we think we are, that we have capacities and potentials beyond what our families and our culture allow us to believe. We can discover this by mindfully remembering stories that struck a chord in childhood and beyond. Allow yourself to include popular stories and even fairy tales.

As an example, I remember the journeys and characters of Harry Potter and of Jane Eyre. Like Harry Potter, Jane Eyre is an unwanted and unloved child, grudgingly taken in by an aunt who has no intention of helping her find her way in the world. When we meet her, she is tucked away behind curtains, imagining the world based on the pictures in a *History of British Birds* and on scraps of fairy tales she hears from a maid, or later from the then-popular novel *Pamela*. In short, the world Jane lives in is very, very limited, but she doesn't *feel* limited. Her awareness of the world and her place in it extends far beyond her immediate surroundings. Do you remember that feeling? I remember being a little girl standing on the shore watching ships with international flags pass by on the St. Lawrence River. Even though I was small, there was something spacious in me that felt connected to those ships that had come all the way across the ocean.

Plain, honest, sincere, artistic, "tenacious of life," Jane Eyre, like Harry Potter—and like many real-life children—knows that she is meant to be part of a much greater, more magical life. In spite of everything, that knowledge is within her. Like Harry, Jane is viciously bullied by a fat spoiled cousin, and she is also wretchedly excluded from the warmth of family—she listens to Christmas parties while shut up in a little cupboard with only a doll to love. By her own admission (told many years past childhood), Jane isn't a sweet child.

She doesn't receive an invitation by owl to a special school that affirms what she knows in her heart to be true—that she is very different inside than those around her judge her to be. She is not whisked away to Hogwarts but to a wretched school called Lowood. And yet she finds in the depth of her misery a capacity for self-awareness and self-acceptance and a sheer spirit that works a kind of magic. Banished to that grim boarding school, abused beyond all endurance, she at last confronts her aunt as children never did in the Victorian age, calling her bad and hard-hearted.

"Ere I had finished this reply, my soul began to expand, to exult with the strangest sense of freedom, of triumph, I ever felt. It seemed as if an invisible bond had burst, and that I had struggled out into unhoped-for liberty."[27] Even though Jane later feels that this act of vengeance was like a sweet but poisonous wine, it is as necessary to her future development as Harry Potter's wild escape from his tormentors with its own dash of sweet revenge (his bully of a cousin is given a pig's tail).

You have to be someone before you can be no one. This seeming paradox, often repeated in Buddhist circles, means that we need to dare to live our lives, to take up space, to express our feelings without holding back, or nothing can be known or transformed. Transformation is not a new thought to think. It is a drama to be lived. It is a process that begins as we dare to open to life, experiencing what it is like to give and receive, to be part of it.

Out walking one winter day, Jane Eyre—who has survived her horrible childhood to become an educated young woman—comes upon the dark and brooding Mr. Rochester. His horse slips on the ice and he sprains his ankle, compelling him to ask her to help him back to his horse. Jane doesn't yet know that Rochester is the master of the estate where she works as a governess, much less the impact he will have on her life. Yet Jane feels that something has changed. "My help had been needed and claimed: I had given it: I was pleased to have done something; trivial, transitory though the deed was, it was yet an active thing, and I was weary of an existence all passive."[28]

The stories of both Harry Potter and spirited young Jane Eyre carry rich evidence of the expansive nature of our true selves. There is a deep wish inside most of us for a larger life. Most children and adolescents sense that they are capable of greatness—that their hearts and minds are capable of embracing the whole world. Allow yourself to think of a story or a film or a series that reminded you of that wish and capacity.

Postscript

THE GOLDEN TICKET

A fake Buddhist monk stopped me on the street in Manhattan one day, offering me peace for the rest of my life. I was running late, so I shook my head no and hurried on. I had no time for peace. Even rushing, I was aware of the irony of the situation. I was literally running away from someone dressed in monastic robes who was smiling and offering me freedom from suffering because I had to get to New York Insight Meditation Center, where I was teaching a course in mindfulness meditation. As phony as he was, there was a contradiction here that demanded attention.

That fake Buddhist monk persisted. He followed me, repeating "Lifetime peace. Lifetime peace." He smiled broadly and I smiled back, both of us walking fast and me shaking my head no. But step by step, the weirdness of the situation, the racewalking away from a ragged pretend monk toward a modern urban Buddhist center, tugged at me like a hand brake. I slowed down more and more, and finally stopped and faced him. He gave me a broad smile. He looked rough, as if he spent a lot of time outdoors. The look in his eyes was shrewd and appraising but also friendly. I stood there for a beat feeling a confusion of emotions: outrage—how dare he impersonate a Buddhist monk—wariness, curiosity, and a vulnerability tinged with shame. He was about to try to sell me peace. But what was I rushing to New York Insight to sell? A path to peace and freedom. I worked for donations, but so did he. And I was selling a path to peace. Was there really a path?

The fake Buddhist monk wasted no time. He held up a picture of a gleaming monastery on a Himalayan mountaintop, pointing at me and nodding, indicating that I could help in the completion of this Shangri-La. He held up an opened black notebook and showed me a long list of names and corresponding donations of twenty or thirty dollars. Smiling, he acted out what he wanted me to do: scribble my name under the last one on the list, after I made a similar suggested donation. Still smiling, I shook my head no again, this time with an extra-firm nod that was meant to convey that I was a seasoned New Yorker and no fool. I knew very well that real Buddhist monastics don't hustle donations like this. They aren't supposed to buy and sell anything, or even accept charitable donations.

I could feel my face and my posture change. I stood taller and narrowed my eyes, as if distancing myself from him. Seeing that he was losing me, the fake monk changed tactics, putting away the donation pad and handing me wooden wrist beads and what looked like a shiny golden ticket. True to his word, the ticket read LIFETIME PEACE and also WORK SMOOTHLY. The other side featured a picture of Guan Yin, Goddess of Compassion, the bodhisattva who hears the cries of the world. He made a hand gesture from me to him, indicating that I should give something back. Really late at this point and realizing that he was not going to give up, I let go of my morally superior stance and gave him the two dollars' change from the coffee I had just bought. In a beat, without a conscious thought, I went from indignant to smiling and bowing along with him. One skinny latte with an extra shot of lifetime peace, please.

As we both rushed off in separate directions, I chuckled over the cute little tale I had to tell my class. I would hold up the golden ticket for them to see. Look at this! Imagine thinking that you could buy a golden ticket that would instantly grant you happiness and peace. But in fact there is a way...

As I punched the buttons of the elevator that would take me up to the Chelsea loft space that was New York Insight Meditation Center, I had an impression of myself from the inside. I was preparing to play the role of teacher, pulling myself up straight and tall, giving myself a little pep talk.

"All the world's a stage," wrote Shakespeare. We all play many parts. Different postures—different selves—are automatically triggered by different conditions. We are endlessly affirming ourselves, our stories and beliefs, endlessly arguing our case in imaginary courtrooms, defending ourselves against pain—especially the pain of being no one in a vast, indifferent world. The Buddha saw that there is no one self. We are pulled this way and that, inhabited by many disparate selves, each with their own memories and momentum. The spiritual teacher George Gurdjieff said that we don't usually see this strange state of affairs because we have "buffers," which he compared to the shock absorbers between train cars.

But sometimes those buffers come down. Just for a moment, we see ourselves as we are—one self giving way to another, a wounded child defended by a posturing teen or a pompous adult. Seeing this unstable, changing state of affairs can make our hearts twist. It also sets us free.

"There is a crack in everything," as Leonard Cohen sang in that gorgeous song *Anthem.* "That's how the light gets in."

There is another way to inhabit the role of teacher, and I land there eventually. I give up trying to be somebody, especially somebody special. I become willing to show up as I really am, vulnerable, changeable, subject to pain and embarrassment. I trust that if I am truly and honestly present to myself and others, at moments the light of presence would shine through.

I entered the big loft space and walked up to the teaching platform, allowing that short walk past rows of students to be a spiritual quest. *Could I be open? Could we as a group move from isolation to connection and freedom? Could we know the groundedness and spaciousness that come with true presence?*

I took my seat beside a big bronze bell and in front of a beautiful stone statue of the historical Buddha, Siddhartha Gautama. I pictured that Buddha in a long line of buddhas stretching back to the beginningless beginning—that Buddhist cosmology derived from the Indian culture of the time. I envisioned all those awakened ones as infinite points of light—a Milky Way of awakening. It relaxed and opened the tight little fist of my ordinary thought, imagining an infinitely vast universe that included bright benevolent forces. But it was the sound of that bell resonating inside me that truly touched my heart, reminding me that I belong to a much larger world.

That bell stopped our forward momentum, sounding depths in us, inviting us to be still and listen with our whole being: body, heart, and mind. The root of *heal* means "to make whole." When we give our lives our whole attention, we remember that we are made to be part of a greater whole.

"Ring the bells that still can ring," sang Leonard Cohen in *Anthem*. "Forget your perfect offering."

In our bones, we know that we are not separate from the great wholeness—the great mystery of life. But how can we come out of the isolation of our thinking and our fear and find our way? Forget striving and come home to the body in the present moment. Remember the experience of being alive.

"I am home in the here and now," Thich Nhat Hanh taught. "I am solid. I am free. In the ultimate I dwell." By the "ultimate," he meant cosmic. "You look into your physical body and you see your cosmic body—the air, the water, the heat, the soil. And you are made of stars."

Bringing the attention home to the sensation of being present in a body, we experience ourselves as living organisms who are part of a greater life—breathing air, touching the earth with our feet, living under a sun that is a star in a vast universe.

The body is a portal. By bringing the attention to the body, we glimpse that we are like waves in the ocean. We are separate forms, and yet we are made of ocean. Realizing this frees us from fear. As limited and alone as we may feel in any given moment, we cannot be separate from the cosmos. We are made of the same stuff—earth, air, fire, water, star matter, and even gold. Trace amounts of that precious element help maintain our joints and transmit electrical signals throughout the body.

Presence shows us that the gold we seek—the world and the belonging we search for—is already here. We are home.

ACKNOWLEDGMENTS

Books are the product of so many causes and conditions and depend on the work of so many that I haven't the space to name them all. I would like to thank everyone at Shambhala Publications, especially Beth Frankl, who took a chance on this book. Thank you also to Samantha Ripley, who worked hard to make it an actual book, and to everyone else at Shambhala who helped bring this into the world.

It feels right to take a step backward and express my gratitude to my parents for the gift of this life, which has contained just enough love and loss, mishap and marvel, grief and grace, to open my heart and mind to the state of awareness called presence.

The family that makes itself known in this book includes my own kin and also my spiritual family and ancestors. I bow to the Buddha and to all who have kept his teachings and practices alive. In my own life, they include the scholar, translator, and teacher Ven. Bhikkhu Bodhi and all those contemporary Buddhist teachers who created the retreat centers and courses of training and books that I have benefited from, among them Jack Kornfield and Sharon Salzberg, who took the time to read and comment on this book.

So many others have enriched my life with their books and teachings. Endless thanks for the teachings of G. I. Gurdjieff and to all those who kept his teachings and work alive, especially Jeanne de Salzmann and Lord John Pentland and all those members of the Gurdjieff Foundation of New York who listened to my questions and encouraged me to believe that I had something to contribute, among them William Segal and Roger Lipsey.

Among my greatest teacher—and beloved spiritual family— are those amazing beings who make up the Hudson River Sangha. During the dark, uncertain days of the pandemic we became virtual and international. Yet we began at the late great Yoga Shivaya in Tarrytown, New York, meditating within sight and sound of the fog horns on the Hudson River, thanks to the generosity of Kathleen Hinge. Thank you also to Westchester Insight and Gina Sharpe, the New York Insight Meditation Center, and the Rubin Museum of Art for offering me the opportunity to teach and tell some of the stories that appear in this book.

Warmest thanks and love to the friends who encouraged me to believe that I had a book in me over the years, including Kent Jones, Mary Ellen O'Neill, Loren Eiferman, and Roger Lipsey, who also contributed a short foreword that I aspire to live up to. Some encouraging friends went so far as to come along on some of the adventures I write about here, including Elizabeth Napp and friends at that wonderful group that call themselves ServiceSpace who invited me to come to India.

I would also like to express my deepest gratitude to all those who took the time to read this book, catch mistakes, and offer their words of endorsement, all of whom have their own important work to do.

I owe my greatest debt of gratitude, however, to my husband, Jeff Zaleski, who has read every word in this book and so many more. Jeff has been there for me, reading and editing, sometimes credulous but supportive, every step of the way. Thank you doesn't begin to cover it. And to my daughter, Alexandra Zaleski, who helped me believe in myself and build this book. Sweetheart, as we've been saying since you were about four years old, we are the team! I'm so grateful to have you in my life.

And to all the benevolent beings unnamed or unseen who have helped me, thank you.

NOTES

1. Rainer Maria Rilke, *Letters to a Young Poet: A New Translation and Commentary*, trans. Anita Barros and Joanna Macy (Boulder: Shambhala Publications, 2021), 70.
2. "The Thanksgiving Prayer," *Parabola* 24, no. 2 (Summer 1999), https://parabola.org/2016/11/24/the-thanksgiving-prayer -adapted-from-the-mohawk. This was originally published as "Thanksgiving Address: Greetings to the Natural World," translated and adapted from the Mohawk by John Stokes and David Kanawahienton Benedict in 1993 with the support of the Six Nations Indian Museum and The Tracking Project.
3. James Boswell, *The Life of Samuel Johnson, LL. D.* (London: n.p., 1823), 3:171.
4. Emily Dickinson, *The Poems of Emily Dickinson*, edited by R.W. Franklin (Cambridge, MA: Belknap Press, 1999), 170.
5. Viktor E. Frankl, *Man's Search for Meaning*, trans. Ilse Sasch (Boston: Beacon Press, 1992), 85.
6. Rainer Maria Rilke, "Let This Darkness Be a Bell Tower," in *In Praise of Mortality: Selections from Duino Elegies and Sonnets to*

Orpheus, trans. Joanna Macy and Anita Barrows (Brattleboro, VT: Echo Point Books and Media, 2016).

7. Carl Gustav Jung, *Memories, Dreams, Reflections*, ed. Aniela Jaffé, trans. Richard Winston and Clara Winston (New York: Vintage Books, 1989), 247.

8. Charles Dickens, *A Christmas Carol and Other Haunting Tales* (New York: Doubleday, 1998), 277–78.

9. P. L. Travers, "The World of the Hero," *Parabola* 1, no. 1 (1976): 47.

10. Quoted in Tara Brach, *Radical Acceptance: Embracing Your Life with the Heart of a Buddha* (New York: Bantam Books, 2004), 36.

11. Meister Eckhart, *The Complete Mystical Works of Meister Eckhart*, trans. Maurice O'Connell Walshe (New York: Crossroad Publishing Company, 2009), 588.

12. Jack Kornfield, *The Wise Heart: A Guide to the Universal Teachings of Buddhist Psychology* (New York: Bantam Books, 2009), 147.

13. Walter Sullivan, "The Einstein Papers, A Man of Many Parts," *The New York Times*, March 29, 1972.

14. Nora Ephron, "Parenting in Three Stages," in *I Feel Bad about My Neck: And Other Thoughts about Being a Woman* (New York: Knopf, 2006).

15. T. S. Eliot, *The Wasteland*, Bloom's Modern Critical Interpretations (New York: Chelsea House, 2007), 21.

16. Harold Brodkey, "Angel," quoted in Nick Paumgarten, "Energy and How to Get It," *The New Yorker*, November 1, 2021.

17. Robert M. Pirsig, *Zen and the Art of Motorcycle Maintenance: An Inquiry into Values* (New York: HarperCollins, 1974), 4–5.

18. Leo Tolstoy, *War and Peace*, trans. Nathan Haskell Dole (New York: Thomas Y. Crowell & Co., 1889), 1:68.

19. Richard Powers, *The Overstory: A Novel* (New York: W. W. Norton and Company, 2018).

20. Powers, *The Overstory*.

21. C. S. Lewis, *The Complete C. S. Lewis Signature Classics* (New York: HarperOne, 2007), 163.

22. Annie Dillard, *Pilgrim at Tinker Creek* (New York: Harper Perennial Modern Classics, 2007).

23. Henry D. Thoreau, *Walden, A Fully Annotated Edition*, ed. Jeffrey S. Cramer (New London, CT: Yale University Press, 2004).

24. Thoreau, *Walden.*

25. Thoreau, *Walden.*

26. Bhikkhu Bodhi, trans., *The Noble Eightfold Path: Way to the End of Suffering* (Onalaska, WA: Pariyatti Publishing, 2000), 13.

27. Charlotte Bronte, *Jane Eyre* (New York: Penguin Classics, 2010), 39.

28. Bronte, *Jane Eyre*, 117.